MATTHEW HALE

Matthew Hale

EDMUND HEWARD

ROBERT HALE · LONDON

ISBN 0 7091 3552 1

Robert Hale & Company
63 Old Brompton Road
London, S.W.7

PRINTED IN GREAT BRITAIN BY
CLARKE, DOBLE & BRENDON LTD.
PLYMOUTH

CONTENTS

ILLUSTRATIONS

PREFACE

Matthew Hale was one of the outstanding judges of the seventeenth century. He was a lawyer of great learning and a fearless judge who resisted all pressures put upon him by Oliver Cromwell and Charles II and could not be solicited by bribes or any other inducements.

The seventeenth century was a period when the overriding political question was the extent of the power of the Sovereign and the limitations which could or should be put upon it. Hale held that the king was bound by his coronation oath to observe the laws of the land and the liberties of the subject. His guiding principle in political matters was not to engage in any party controversy and during the Civil War he helped the Royalists with money and advice and after the Restoration tried to shield Quakers and Dissenters from the rigours of the laws enacted to suppress them. Although he did not take part in politics, he was a public figure sitting on committees for law reform, trade and church unity and advising the King and his Ministers on legal matters.

Many of Hale's actions can only be understood in the light of his deeply-held religious convictions. His outstanding quality was integrity. A man should adhere strictly to all contracts freely made and above all keep his oath. He should speak the truth and deal honestly and justly with his neighbours. When he became a judge he was particularly scrupulous not to accept or appear to accept presents and made a practice of paying more for an article than it was worth so that he could not be accused of using his position for his own ends. When in the country he paid beggars to pile up stones to make roads, but when in London he gave to every beggar who asked of him on the grounds that one out of ten might be genuine and this man would be missed unless he gave to all. He was a devout member of the Church of England but was not much concerned with the niceties of religious observance and had the disconcerting habit of standing up in church whenever the Scriptures were read, whatever the rest of the congregation was doing. It was the practice for men to be buried in church and for the most important ones to be buried near the altar. He disapproved, holding that churches were for the living and church-yards for the dead.

Hale had an impetuous and passionate temper which he kept under strict control. He ate and drank sparingly but was a heavy smoker. He was careless of his appearance, dressing in the style in fashion when he was thirty years old and thinking that black was the most suitable colour for country wear. In his youth he had been an excellent fencer but he took no part in field sports as he did not approve of killing animals for pleasure. His old horses were put out to pasture and every animal was entitled to live its natural life.

He had many of the prejudices of an Englishman. He did not travel abroad, disliked foreigners and saw no point in learning foreign languages, the classics excepted. He was very interested in foreign trade and the balance of payments but opposed the unlimited entry of foreigners into the country. He did not care for music or the visual arts and, although he was interested in building, his knowledge of architecture was rudimentary. He was infected with the intellectual excitement of his time, enjoying the friendship of many of the founders of the Royal Society and dabbling in scientific experiments himself. He was a prudent man of business, investing in land and providing by means of settle-ments in his lifetime for all the members of his family.

Hale was an extremely thorough and accurate lawyer and it was this thoroughness which took him back to the sources of the law. During the course of his researches he became a legal historian and some of his knowledge he passed on to students in his books on the common law. There is a clarity about his writing which was the result of his orderly thinking. Before starting on any enterprise he liked to have a plan, and this applied to his writing. He never sat down to write for publication but used writing as a method of setting down his thoughts on a particular issue. If he was asked his opinion it was committed to writing; notes on the practice and procedure of the courts were jotted down on paper; religious meditation was written down as an aid to concentration.

He saw clearly how the law gets out of date and requires re-newing and compared the law with the Argonauts' ship "which was the same when it returned home as it was when it went out, though in that long voyage it had successive amendments and scarce came back with any of its former materials". He can be regarded as one of our foremost law reformers. He suggested the formation of the Law Commission three hundred years before it was established in 1965, and by his writings on law reform and service on the Hale Commission of 1652 he suggested many reforms which have since been put into effect.

As a judge Hale had quickness of apprehension, an exact memory, was courteous and patient with witnesses and members of the Bar and, unlike so many judges of his time, did not browbeat those giving evidence. He thought time was well spent in arriving at the truth and engraved in Latin on his staff was the motto "More haste less speed." He did not think that it was for a judge to make law as this would be usurping the functions of Parliament. He had a great respect for the law, holding himself to be bound by his oath as a judge to administer justice in accordance with law.

Hale's legal influence does not lie in his judgments but in his statements of the existing law contained in such books as *The History of the Pleas of the Crown*, which were learned, authoritative and complete and in the maintenance of the highest standards in his professional life and work.

I am indebted in particular to Professor Harry Hollond who has read the manuscript and given much help and advice. I also wish to acknowledge with gratitude the assistance given to me in many different ways by the Benchers and Librarian of Lincoln's Inn, the staff of the London Library and the Gloucester Records Office, Mary Cotterell, David Yale, Michael Prichard, Mathew Hale, James Lees-Milne, Donald Veall, Hazel Rowland and my wife.

Royal Courts of Justice EDMUND HEWARD
March 1972

I

Early Life 1609-28

The village of Alderley lies two miles south of Wotton-under-Edge in the county of Gloucester. It is wedged between two brooks, the Ozleworth and the Kilcott, underneath Winner Hill, and in the sixteenth and seventeenth centuries it contained a number of woollen mills. Wotton was at that time a centre of the woollen industry, and it is said that there were fifteen mills along the Ozleworth and another five along the Kilcott.[1] It was here that Matthew Hale was born on 1st November 1609.[2]

On his father's side Hale's ancestry can be traced back to his great grandfather, Robert Hale of Dursley, who died in 1585. His grandfather, also named Robert, was a prosperous clothier at Wotton, lord of the manor of Rangeworthy and married Alice Crew of Alderley on 27th March 1570.[3] He acquired a fortune of £10,000 and after providing portions for his daughters divided his estate among his sons. His second son, Robert, was Matthew Hale's father.[4] The family tradition of rectitude can be found in Hale's grandfather. In the survey of Wotton Manor taken on 1st July 1573, when the Hundred of Wotton was established at the instance of the Earls of Leicester and Berkeley, it is recorded that four of the jurymen refused to consent to an untrue present-ment on one point and were accordingly struck off the panel. One of the four jurymen was Robert Hale of Wotton, but un-fortunately we do not know what the untrue presentment was about.[5] We can also trace in him the tradition of charity to the poor, as in 1578 he left a rentcharge of 20s. in North Nibley "for the poorest inhabitants".[6]

On his mother's side Hale was descended from the very ancient family of Poyntz, who came to England with William the Conqueror and settled at Iron Acton near Bristol. Some members of the family became established in Alderley, and in the sixteenth century the names of Poyntz, Crew and Webb are constantly re-curring in the Alderley parish registers. Hale's mother Joan, daughter of Matthew Poyntz of Alderley, was baptized in Alderley parish church on 29th September 1577.[7]

Matthew's father, Robert, matriculated at Broadgates Hall Oxford on 28th April 1580 aged 17 years[8] and, being a member of Lincoln's Inn, was called to the bar on 5th February 1594.[9] He was extremely scrupulous, and it was on account of his scruples that he gave up practice at the Bar. He could not bring himself to accept the rules of pleading which he thought to be dishonest and retired to his home in Alderley. The only known portrait of Robert shows a face of great sensitivity, and he was clearly a man of principle with intelligence and a gentle nature. It can be argued that it was a sign of weakness not to accept life as it was and to withdraw from his profession, but on the other hand it might be said that he had the intelligence to see the weaknesses in the practice of the law, and principles strong enough not to accept them. In the practice of the law rules which are laid down for the sake of convenience and which are admirable in themselves at the time become outdated with changing circumstances and social conditions and quickly become impediments to the pursuit of justice. It was only strong judges who could have altered the situation, and Robert, being powerless to do anything about it, withdrew to the country. Robert married Matthew's mother Joan Poyntz at Alderley on 13th September 1599,[10] when he was about 36 years of age. In the first years of their married life there were no children. It is not known where they originally set up home, but in 1608 they built a house now known as Alderley Grange.[11] This house has a fine situation facing west with long views over the plain and was enlarged in the eighteenth century, when a splendid staircase and beautiful Georgian front were added. Robert may have built the house with a view to his retirement from the bar.

Matthew was the only child of Robert Hale and Joan Poyntz and was born soon after they moved into their new house at Alderley Grange. John Aubrey says that he was born in the evening of 1st November 1609 and that "when his mother fell in labour his father was offering his evening sacrifice".[12] Whether or not his father was in fact saying his prayers at the time of birth, the child was baptized in Alderley parish church on 5th November 1609.[13] Matthew's mother died on 13th April 1612 and was buried at Alderley on 23rd April 1612.[14] His father was left with a child under $2\frac{1}{2}$ years old and he died in 1614. He was not buried at Alderley, but in his will Matthew Hale says that his father died at Alderley Grange. Robert was generous in his giving and on his death Burnet says that he left a small estate worth only about £100 a year out of which £20 per annum was earmarked for the poor of Wotton, who received no assistance from the parish. He made this distinction as the rich were by law bound to pay rates to relieve the poor of the parish and to give to them would only benefit the rich. Robert Hale's charity still exists and, until the land was sold, consisted of cottage, gardens and land adjoining containing 41 acres 1 rood 10 perches of land at Rangeworthy.[15]

There appears to have been a dispute between his father's relatives and his mother's about Matthew's guardianship. His mother's brother, Thomas Poyntz, claimed guardianship but it was eventually agreed that the nearest relative on his father's side, Anthony Kingscot of Kingscot, should be guardian. Great care was taken with his education and it was hoped that he would become a clergyman in the Church of England. He was thoroughly grounded by Mr Stainton, the vicar of Wotton, a Puritan minister, and at a very early age his ability was apparent.

In 1626, when he was 16 years old, Hale was sent to Magdalen Hall Oxford, where his tutor was Obadiah Sedgewick, then aged 26. Sedgewick was not the most concilatory of men and when a lecturer at St. Mildred's Bread Street was censured for preaching against the episcopacy. He was, by turn, don, army chaplain, parish priest and man of property. Hale's guardian had done all he could to ensure that he continued the Puritan education begun under Mr Stainton.

There is no evidence of his reading at Oxford save that he is said to have told an enquirer that at Oxford he had read Aquinas, Scotus, Suarez and others whom he mentioned. His disposition was naturally gay and ardent and he seems to have reacted against the strictness of his upbringing at Wotton-under-Edge and enjoyed Oxford life to the full. He appears to have acquired a passion for the theatre, spending all his money in this way. He took great pains over his appearance, wearing fine clothes and taking a full part in all social activities. He was physically strong and well proportioned and enjoyed sport and physical exercise. He was an excellent fencer and became so good that he was able to beat his instructors. One of his instructors said that he could teach him no more, so Hale bet him the house in which he lived that he, the instructor, could not hit him on the head. The instructor was in fact a better fencer and won the bet.

While Hale was in this state of mind a career in the Church offered few attractions, and he seriously considered becoming a soldier and joining his tutor Sedgewick, who was accompanying Sir Horatio Vere to the Low Countries as chaplain. Circumstances prevented him taking this course as he became involved in a law suit with Sir William Whitmore, who claimed part of his estate. His guardian was not a man of business, so Hale left Oxford after three years and went to London to look after his own interests. He was recommended to consult a barrister, John Glanville, who became a Serjeant nine years later. Glanville qualified as an attorney but was called to the bar by Lincoln's Inn in his middle twenties. He was Member of Parliament for Plymouth for many years and was Recorder of Bristol. His wife came from Barnsley in Gloucestershire, and it may have been on account of this Gloucestershire connection that Hale was introduced to Glanville. Although Hale was only 19 at the time, Glanville observed his ability and quick grasp of the facts and legal principles involved. He advised and encouraged him to take up the law as his career, and on 8th November 1628[16] Hale was admitted a student at Lincoln's Inn.

To begin with he continued the same way of living, enjoying the company of his friends and joining them in their pleasures. One evening he went out of town with a party of friends. During the evening one of them became so drunk that he passed out and the others thought he was going to die. Fortunately the friend recovered, but the effect on Hale was in the nature of a sudden conversion. He vowed that he would never drink another health during his life, which vow he kept, even refusing to drink the King's health despite pressure from his friends.

From this time onwards he worked sixteen hours a day, later reducing it to eight hours a day. In old age he advised six hours a day, saying that he thought "to fix six hours a day with attention and constancy, was sufficient; that a man must use his body as he would use his horse and his stomach, not tire him at once but rise with an appetite." He began dressing in a very plain manner, and his style of dress got him into trouble. On one occasion he was seized by a press gang, who, seeing that he was strong and able bodied, thought he would be an excellent recruit for the navy. He was only released after long explanations, and after this he seems to have dressed a little better. Throughout his life friends were constantly chiding him about his appearance, and for a time he would take notice and then relapse again. One day he was buying cloth for a new suit and was arguing with the draper about the price. The draper offered the cloth to him for nothing if he would promise him £100 when he became Lord Chief Justice of England. He replied that he could not with a good conscience wear any man's cloth unless he paid for it. Hale had very definite views about clothes. A man's clothing should be clean and decent and not costly.[17] He makes the interesting remark that you can no longer distinguish the quality of a person by his clothing. Clothes should be made from English broadcloth and for summer from stuffs made in England, as at Norwich. He did not approve of kersies, serge, silk or satin, or gold and silver lace. For women he grudgingly admits that silk may be worn sometimes provided it is English, but for ordinary wear they should use English stuff. On no account should they wear silver or gold nor costly rich bone laces made overseas, nor foreign and outlandish silks.

When Hale was about 30 years of age he decided the fashion of suit he would wear and stuck to it for the remainder of his life. The reasoning was that by that age a man should have outgrown the vanities of youth, of which following the fashion was one. He did not like light-coloured clothes such as red, blue and green, but thought that they should be sad coloured. Black is most decent but always seasonable especially in the country. Finally he advises warm clothing, especially in the winter and spring.

Hale was a tall, well-built man, strong both physically and mentally, with the power to put into action the decisions he had made. He had a quick brain, a good memory, great industry, and was very exact and thorough. He was naturally impetuous and given to excess but was ready to learn from experience. He had exceptional powers of self-control for a man with such a passionate nature.

Hale read the life of T. Pomponius Atticus by Cornelius Nepos and was deeply impressed by what he read. He resolved to model himself on Atticus, and consequently the life of Atticus had a great bearing on the life and conduct of Hale.

Titus Pomponius Atticus, born in 109 B.C., was a member of one of the most ancient equestrian families in Rome and the son of a wealthy and enlightened father. He was given a liberal education and was 21 years of age when the civil war broke out. He decided to take no part in the war, withdrawing to Athens with most of his movable property under the pretext of continuing his studies and remaining there for twenty-three years. He was content with his equestrian rank and did not seek any public employment or honours, nor did he join any political party. He kept on good terms with members of all parties, numbering amongst his friends Caesar, Pompey, Brutus, Cassius and Octavianus, whilst his most intimate friend was Cicero.

Atticus assisted his friends of whatever party with gifts or loans of money when they required it. He was very wealthy, as his father left 2,000,000 sesterces, and he invested large sums

B

in various corporations which farmed the public revenue. His wide business interests ranged from banking to publishing, and he had a large number of carefully educated slaves whom he employed in transcribing books. When in Athens he purchased a large estate in Epirus, but for the most part he lived quietly in a modest house in the Quirinal in Rome, which was a well-known literary centre.

Hale made an English translation of the rather fulsome life of Atticus by Cornelius Nepos with some notes.[18] The translation was not very felicitous, and he apologizes that it does not run as smoothly as he could have wished but that it was a literal translation. In the notes he comments on various aspects of the life of Atticus, analyzing his methods of self-preservation under two general heads, firstly his care to avoid making enemies, and secondly his endeavour to make all men his friends. Under the first head he was careful not to accept too many benefits from great men, particularly those whom he could not repay. He contented himself with his condition in life, which was comfortable enough, and had no ambition to become a great man. He was modest and did not expect undue respect or attention from others. He overlooked the injuries he suffered but remembered the benefits he received from other men. This course of conduct enabled him to preserve his liberty as he was not beholden to any man nor was he a source of envy.

One method adopted by Atticus to avoid becoming involved in faction was to avoid public office in the State. He would do everything in his power for individuals or the State as a private person, but public office emoluments and honours are coveted by most men, and a man who accepts them is the subject of envy. Hale comments on the folly of men who voluntarily undertake the burdens and dangers of great office and remarks on the wisdom of Greece where men had to be compelled to take public office. Besides being the subject of envy, a man who undertakes public office loses all the quiet and tranquillity of private life. Any faults which he may have are exposed to the glare of publicity, and even minor mistakes are the subject of talk and gossip which can cloud great abilities and achievements. His mistakes will be more far reaching in their effect than those made by a private citizen and his errors of judgment may affect thousands. Finally nobody can take office and exercise power effectively without making enemies. By avoiding public office Atticus enjoyed a peaceful life, improving his knowledge and learning; he avoided making enemies as no one envied him; he retained his safety and his reputation; and it enabled him to use his good offices with the party in power for the benefit of his friends in the opposite faction.

He took the greatest pain to avoid being the subject of envy. Not only did he refuse public office but refused to have a statue erected in his honour and, although he came into money from his uncle, he did not change his manner of living nor increase his expenditure. Although he was rich he avoided the reputation of lavish expenditure by keeping his expenses low and keeping the possessions bequeathed to him by his father and uncle. Hale writes: "In short he kept such a mediocrity in his house, his furniture, his household expenses, his entertainments and the manner of his living, that neither exposed him to scorn on the one hand, nor censure, or envy, or imputation of affecting either too much grandeur and popularity nor on the other hand consumed or wasted his estate."

Atticus never made any public accusation against any man nor did he engage in any private litigation of any kind. He preferred to forgive injuries rather than go to law. He guarded his tongue and conducted himself with consideration for others without pride or haughtiness. Hale comments that it is a common mistake of great men to think themselves above the reach of enemies and to make enemies needlessly by their insolence. He tells a story of a mouse who troubled the sleeping lion and happened to fall under the lion's paw. The mouse begged for mercy and told the lion that he might possibly be of assistance to the lion in the future. The lion let him go and later the mouse was able to gnaw through the net in which the lion was entangled. "Kindness and affability and gentleness are but cheap and easy things and as easily exercised as roughness and acerbity."

On the positive side of making friends Atticus was liberal to his many friends, especially to those in distress. He gave with no thought of return, as in his distribution of corn to the poor of Athens, his relief of Marcus, Pompey, Brutus and the family of Antony when in desperate need.

Hale praised Atticus for the moderation and equability of his mind and actions saying, "One of the greatest enemies of any man's peace and safety is the immoderation and excess of passion which ordinarily carries men into excesses and extremes, and creates enemies and troubles if it finds none . . . but our worthy person was quite of another make; he governed his passions and thereby governed his actions and speeches, was deliberate and considerate, and of great moderation."

At the age of 77 years Atticus fell ill and for three months suffered no great pain. At the end of this time the disease suddenly became very active and painful. It appeared to be incurable and Atticus sent for his son-in-law Agrippa and told him that his end was near and that he had decided to hasten his death which was inevitable. He sought Agrippa's approval and asked him not to try and dissuade him as his mind was made up. Agrippa wept and besought him not to carry out this plan, but to no avail. After Atticus had fasted for two days his fever left him and on the fifth day he died.

Hale is eulogistic about Atticus, but he has one reservation as he considered that his failure to take nourishment prior to his death was not at all commendable "as it savoured too much of impatience, unbecoming a philosopher, so it was an act of much wilful imprudence, for the receiving of convenient nourishment might prolong his life and possibly abate his pain".

Hale resolved that he also would not engage in faction nor meddle in any public business, and would help his friends of whatever party when in need. During the Civil War he aided Royalists financially, and after the Restoration as a judge he assisted Dissenters who were being oppressed by the King's party. He did, however, take public office as a judge both under Cromwell and Charles II.

Hale was educated by Puritans and in order to understand his character it is necessary to understand something about the Puritan tradition.

The Puritans were opposed to outward observances at church services, such as the use of the cross at baptism, the cap and surplice, the ring in marriage, and bowing at the name of Jesus. On the other hand they taught that examination should precede communion, that the Lord's Day should be strictly observed, that church music should be moderated and the service shortened. They held that only men capable of preaching should be appointed as ministers, that non-residence be forbidden, and that the clergy should be permitted to marry. They disapproved of plurality of livings and thought that excommunication should be sparingly used.

Puritanism has been defined by George Trevelyan as "the religion of those who wished either to purify the image of the Established Church from the taint of Papacy, or to worship separately by forms so purified". Hale throughout his life was a loyal member of the Church of England and, therefore, comes within the first category. When he was young there was great discontent with the state of the Church and young men from the universities seeking appointments in the Church saw no hope save in Puritanism. The strength of the Establishment was against any reforms and Puritans turned to preaching either as lecturers or as parish ministers. The main body of Puritan ministers never lost hope of establishing a Presbyterian system within the Church of England, whilst the remainder were the Independents or Congregationalists who became the first Dissenters. Not only did the Puritans preach, but they wrote books telling men what to believe and how to act. They taught that the will of God was revealed in the Bible, in the human heart and in nature, but their basic premise was the depravity of man.

Before embarking on any enterprise Hale would prepare a plan of action. Burnet copied from the original a scheme which he prepared for the use of time which clearly shews Puritan influence.

Morning

1. To lift up the heart to God in thankfulness for renewing my life.
2. To renew my covenant with God in Christ
   (1) By renewed acts of faith receiving Christ and rejoicing in the height of that relation.
   (2) Resolution of being one of his people, doing him allegiance.
3. Adoration and prayer.
4. Saving a watch over my own infirmities and passions, over the snares laid down in our way Perimus licitis [we are ruined by indulgence].

Day Employment

There must be an employment, two kinds
1. Our ordinary calling, to serve God in it. It is service to Christ, though never so mean—Collos 3 Here faithfulness, diligence, cheerfulness. Not to overlay myself with more business than I can bear.
2. Our spiritual employments, mingle somewhat of God's immediate service in this day.

Refreshments

1. Meat and drink in moderation seasoned with somewhat of God.
2. Recreations. 1. Not our business. 2. Suitable. No games, if given to covetousness or passion.

If Alone

1. Beware of wandering, vain, lustful thoughts; fly from thyself rather than entertain these.
2. Let thy solitary thoughts be profitable; view the evidence of thy salvation, the state of thy soul, the coming of Christ, thy own mortality, it will make thee humble and watchful.

Company

Do good to them. Use God's name reverently. Beware of leaving an ill impression of ill example. Receive good from them, if more knowing.

Evening

Cast up the accounts of the day. If ought amiss, beg pardon. Gather resolution of more vigilance. If well, bless the mercy and grace of God that hath supported thee.

Throughout his life Hale ate and drank sparingly. Breakfast consisted of a crust of bread and a draught of beer or ale as he considered that eating much in the morning clouded the brain.[19] The main meal of the day was dinner, between 11 a.m. and 1 p.m., with a light supper between 6 and 7 p.m. It was necessary to get up from a meal with an appetite and never allow more than one hour for your dinner if you had any choice. He disapproved of French cooking and said French meals were twelve times as expensive as English meals. So far as drink was concerned you should not take more than three moderate draughts of beer at mealtimes or one or two small draughts of wine if your stomach required it. Nothing should be drunk between dinner and supper or between supper and going to bed. Sack should be drunk sparingly, a small glass before a meal and a small glass afterwards, but not by young people under 30 years of age. Strong waters, brandies and aqua-vitae should never be drunk except as a medicine. "I have known many men especially such as were strong, young and full of blood taken away even while they have been excessively drinking strong waters." Hale made it a rule never to go into a tavern or ale house unless it was on necessary business, as on a journey or a meeting of Justices of the Peace.

With regard to sleeping, Hale went to bed at 10 p.m. rising at 6 a.m. and in any event not later than 7 a.m.[20] Those in good health should have six hours sleep and not more than eight hours. The young and healthy should not sleep in the daytime. For old men and those who cannot sleep at night a nap in the daytime was permissible.

Hale was a heavy smoker and many bills for tobacco still exist: for example, a bill dated 20th July 1661 for 4 pounds of tobacco 12s.[21] He rationalized his addiction by saying that, as he had a cold complexion and constitution, tobacco had been a great preservative of his health.[22] He had qualms about recommending tobacco to his grandchildren and begged them not to follow his example. He thought it permissible to take a very little if you were over 30 years of age and your health permitted, but it was better not to smoke at all. If you did smoke, he advised taking it an hour after dinner and an hour after supper, but said that it took a great deal or resolution not to smoke to excess in the course of time.

Apart from fencing at Oxford, he was fond of walking in the countryside. His main recreations were, however, intellectual, and he turned with pleasure to the study of philosophy, religion, history and natural sciences. Burnet says that he made a good collection of very excellent instruments, sparing no cost to have them as exact as art could make them, but unfortunately he does not say what the instruments were. He bequeathed a book on optics to Lincoln's Inn so they may have been optical instruments.

He appears to have had the Puritan distrust of music as a sensual pleasure and there is no indication that he had any interest in the visual arts. He saw no object in the study of modern languages, and this is merely a symptom of his insularity. He did not approve of foreign food, foreign clothes or foreign people. He did not think that foreign laws could be adapted for the use of English people. He was proficient in Latin, as almost all learning was written in Latin, but he never travelled abroad.

He was fond of building, but it is doubtful whether he would have made a good architect as his attitude to architecture was altogether too utilitarian. Alderley is near Badminton, where the Duke of Beaufort was building Badminton House. Hale paid him a visit and made an unsolicited suggestion: "to have one door to his house, and the window of his study, where he sat, must open upon that". The reasoning behind the suggestion was that even the greatest of men should be economical as this was the way to preserve their fortunes. There is a plan of a house with the papers at the Record Office, Gloucester, which is clearly drawn by Hale himself with the door in the middle, rectangular in shape, with the front rooms on each flank projecting a little and the two rear rooms forming the sides of a courtyard.

He was always very conscious of the dangers of day dreaming and idle thoughts, and he used to set aside time every Sunday for religious meditation. To prevent his thoughts from wandering he would commit them to paper. This is the reason why his writing on religious subjects is so voluminous. They were not intended for publication, but were the mechanics of meditation.

To return to his career, a decision had now to be made about his future. Apparently his father in his will had expressed the wish that he should follow the law, but he came down from Oxford with an aversion to lawyers, thinking them "a barbarous sort of people unfit for anything but their own trade". To his surprise he found Glanville both prudent and generous with a breadth of mind which he admired, and he often acknowledged his debt to Glanville for introducing him to the law.

NOTES

1 James Lees-Milne, "A Village of Fine Houses", *Country Life*, 3rd July 1969.

2 Alderley parish registers. In the baptismal register the spelling of Hale's Christian name is Matthew while in the register of burials it is spelt Mathew. Hale is said to have been named after his grandfather, Matthew Poyntz, who spelt his name Matthew. Family tradition has it that the spelling should be Mathew. As Hale has always been known as Matthew Hale this spelling has been preferred.

3 Alderley parish registers.

4 The main source of personal details is Burnet's *Life of Sir Matthew Hale and John Earl of Rochester*. It would be tedious to give references for every piece of information taken from Burnet and it can be assumed that the information comes from Burnet unless a reference is given to the contrary.

5 E. S. Lindley, *Wotton-under-Edge*, p. 38.

6 ibid.

7 Alderley parish registers.

8 Joseph Foster, *Alumni Oxoniensis 1500–1714*, vol. II.

9 Admission book, Lincoln's Inn.

10 Alderley parish registers.

11 Now the home of Mr and Mrs James Lees-Milne.

12 John Aubrey, *Brief Lives*, vol. I, p. 278.

13 Alderley parish registers.

14 ibid.

15 Taken from statements of Wotton-under-Edge Charities, 1892.

16 Admission book, Lincoln's Inn.

17 Letters to his grandchildren, ch. 20, p. 95, B. M. Harl MS. 4009. Hale's views on clothing are taken from this chapter.

18 Sir Matthew Hale, *The Life of Pomponius Atticus*, London, 1677. (Also published in *The Works moral and religious of Sir Matthew Hale*, London, 1805, edited by the Rev. T. Thirlwall, vol. I, p. 423.)

19 Letters to his grandchildren, ch. 19, p. 89. B. M. Harl MS. 4009.

20 ibid., p. 92.

21 Bills in Public Record Office, Gloucester.

22 Letters to his grandchildren, ch. 19, p. 91.

II

The Bar 1629-51

Hale was admitted a student by Lincoln's Inn on 8th November 1628[1] and called to the bar on 17th May 1636.[2] On admission he became a pupil of William Noy. Noy was a Cornishman born in 1577 and educated at Exeter College, Oxford. He was a very hard worker and a sound lawyer with a good memory and knowledge of the law. In his early days he was a Parliamentarian, and it caused some surprise when he was appointed Attorney-General to Charles I in 1631. As the King's Attorney it was his duty to support the King's interest, and the appointment was a shrewd one from the King's point of view. Noy was most assiduous in the performance of his duties, taking every point in the King's favour and carrying out all his instructions with care, energy, and determination. He was also a great supporter of the Church of England, and Archbishop Laud said that Noy was the best friend the Church ever had of a layman.

Being in chambers with Noy meant that Hale became acquainted with many of the leading Royalists, and during his early years he gained a substantial practice as a conveyancer, drawing settlements for noble families. His friendship with Noy was such that he became known as 'Young Noy'.

Many of his ideas about practice at the bar were unconventional but were the result of his religious faith. For example, if a man had a bad case he refused to act and advised the client to find another counsel. He would not have approved of the principle of 'the cab-rank', that it was the duty of counsel to present the case of anyone who asked so that everybody should have the opportunity of having his case put in the best possible light and all arguments in his favour properly presented and canvassed. Men in the seventeenth century were more direct both in their language and actions, and the idea of actively defending a bad man or presenting a case with no merit appeared to be immoral. As Hale gained experience he modified his ideas, as he found that on occasion, owing to the ignorance of the client or neglect of the attorney in preparing the case, he had not sufficient facts upon which to base an opinion and further investigation showed that the client had a good case. If a client had a weak case he always advised a settlement.

On the subject of advocacy, he was careful always to keep strictly to the truth and to be short and to the point. This is rather unexpected as in his writing he is copious, covering every possible point. He had a distrust of eloquence and oratory and thought that facts should speak for themselves. He said "if a judge or jury had a right understanding it signified nothing but a waste of time and loss of words; and if they were weak and easily wrought on it was a more decent way of corrupting them by bribing their fancies and biassing their affections".

He expressed surprise that French lawyers should model themselves on the Roman orators, as the purpose of Roman oratory was to persuade in the context of city politics and public affairs. In Hale's view it was not the function of counsel to persuade the court but to state all the facts and the law, clearly and concisely, to help the court reach the right decision and to do justice. This should be done with the minimum of words. In the eighteenth century Lord Mansfield studied the orators of Rome with the object of learning how to persuade, and in the nineteenth century the power of eloquence and oratory was used with great effect by the most famous advocates. The rather dry and factual approach to advocacy of our own time is a return to the methods of Hale.

While he did not admire a slavish imitation of Roman orators, Hale had a great admiration for Roman law as a system. He preferred the English trial system of juries, but with his scientific turn of mind he found Roman law congenial. Burnet reports: "He often said that the true grounds and reasons of law were so well delivered in the digests that a man could never understand law as a science so well as by seeking it there, and therefore lamented much that it was so little studied in England." He compares the early Briton unfavourably with the Roman saying: "the Britains were not reduced to that civilized estate as to keep the annals and memorials of their laws and government as the Romans and other civilized parts of the world have done".[3] Roman law provided a basis of comparison for Hale from which he could judge the common law and suggest improvements. Undoubtedly his knowledge of Roman law and its methods of arrangement provided the background to his attempt to classify the common law in his *The Analysis of the Law.*

He greatly admired one aspect of the Roman system: that in Rome certain jurists were men of the highest standing bred to take office in the State and who mastered the law as part of their equipment for office. These men gave their opinions to all freely thinking it below them to take any fee for their advice. The republican jurists defined the law by making general propositions from the material of previous decisions. As Peter Stein says, they "saw their role as that of declaring the pre-existing law and defining its precise limits in a scientific way".[4]

It is recorded that Hale did not take the full profits of his practice at the bar. In an ordinary case he would return one half of the usual fee, and in a straightforward case which did not require much study he had a standard fee of 10s. When he became established in practice his services were often sought to act as arbitrator, but although he frequently acted he would not accept a fee. This was a cause of embarrassment to those who instructed him, but he took the line that an arbitrator was in fact a judge, and a judge should accept no fee. There are two rather interesting documents at the Record Office, Gloucester, one an original deed of annuity dated 26th April 1650 from the Governor of Charterhouse to Hale for £5 per annum for his services as counsel, and another dated 10th October 1653 from the mayor and burgesses of the City of Gloucester for £2 per annum for his good counsel and advice. In the fourteenth century barristers and physicians were often paid by means of an annuity, presumably because of lack of capital, and the practice appears to have continued until the seventeenth century, at any rate so far as corporations were concerned.[5]

Being in Noy's chambers and having become well known to Royalists as a conveyancer, it is not surprising that Hale was briefed for many famous Royalist prisoners when at the bar. He appeared as junior counsel for the defence with John Herne at the trial of Archbishop Laud.[6] Laud was accused of endeavouring to subvert the fundamental laws of England, the true Protestant religion and the privileges of Parliament, and on 11th October 1643 John Herne and Hale attended at the House of Lords. Laud in his autobiography says: "John Herne (who was the man that spoke what all had resolved) delivered his argument very freely and stoutly, proving that nothing which I have either said or done according to their charge is treason by any known established law of this kingdom." Counsel for the prosecution, Serjeant Wild, argued that they did not allege that any one crime of Laud's amounted to treason or a felony but that all the Bishop's misdemeanours put together did by way of accumulation, make many treasons. To which Herne tartly replied, "I crave your mercy, good Mr Serjeant. I never understood before this time that two hundred couple of black rabbits would make a black horse."

In the following year Hale appeared as counsel for Connor Lord Macquire.[7] He is only once mentioned in the report with Mr Twisden and nothing is said about his arguments. On 11th November 1644 Lord Macquire was brought before the Court of King's Bench on a charge that he with others did on 20th October 1641 at Dublin in Ireland make an insurrection against the King. About the end of October 1641, when the King was in Scotland, "the most barbarous and bloody rebellion" occurred in Ireland. Protestants were evicted from their estates and over 200,000 men, women and children were murdered in one month. The plot against the Government, concerted with great secrecy, was to be put into operation on 23rd October 1641. Dublin Castle, the headquarters of the government forces and stores, was to be seized by the rebels by nine o'clock on that day and many Irish gentry were ordered to be in Dublin the night before to be in readiness for the attack. Surprise attacks were also planned on all the government forts and strong points in Ireland. The leader of the attack on Dublin Castle was Hugh MacMahon, who on his arrival on the evening of the 22nd October went into a tavern for a drink. He met there one Owen Conally, an Irishman but a Protestant in the service of Sir John Chilworthy, an English M.P. During the course of drinking MacMahon disclosed his plans to Conally, who, escaping from the tavern, went straight to Lord Justice Parsons, whom he saw at 9 p.m. that evening. MacMahon was arrested and examined and so was Lord Macquire. Dublin Castle was put in a state of readiness and many of the principal conspirators, hearing of the arrests, left Dublin during the night and escaped capture. Although the plot was foiled in Dublin it was too late to stop the insurrection in other parts of the country.

When Charles I was brought to trial Hale is said to have advised him to make the plea that the court had no jurisdiction to try him. The trial started on 9th January 1649 and there is no mention of Hale in the State Trials Report. It is likely, however, that he was concerned in advising the King behind the scenes. He had acted for many Royalists and was now, at 40, a man of standing in his profession.

Hale was at this time concerned with the defence of the Duke of Hamilton. When Charles I was executed the Duke of Hamilton was in prison and made an attempt to escape from Windsor with the help of his faithful servant, Cole. Cole arranged to send a servant with two horses to Windsor and the Duke made his escape at night just before the gates were shut. He met his servant with the horses at the place fixed without any alarm being given. It was Cole's plan that the Duke should not arrive in London until seven in the morning, when he would be met and taken by Cole to a safe hiding place in the City. The Duke was unaccustomed to the routine of escape, ignored Cole's instructions, and went direct to Mr Owen's house in Southwark during the night. A party of soldiers were searching Southwark for Sir Lewis Dyver and meeting the Duke at 4 a.m. in the morning stopped and questioned him. The Duke made some plausible excuse and all might have gone well if he had not chosen this moment to light his pipe with some documents he wished to destroy. This was his downfall and he was arrested and held in custody at St James's Palace.

The Duke of Hamilton's trial started on 9th February 1649.[8] He was charged with levying war against the people on behalf of the King on or about 19th July 1648 and in particular that he did fight against the forces of Parliament at Preston on 20th August 1648. On Saturday 10th February the Duke applied for counsel and was asked whether he would name the counsel or wished the court to appoint them. He tried to find his own counsel, but on 13th February he appeared again before the court to say that no counsel would appear for him without an order of the court. At the request of the Duke the court nominated Mr Chute, Mr Hale, Mr Parsons and Dr Walker as his counsel and they were granted free access to the Duke in prison.

The gist of the argument for the defence was that the Duke, being a Scotsman, was only carrying out the orders of the Parliament of his own country, Scotland. His allegiance was to Scotland and not to England and consequently in the circumstances there could be no treason to England. The Duke's father was naturalized in England after the Duke's birth, but it was argued that no man could be the subject of two kingdoms and in his case the Duke was a subject of Scotland. In fact he would have suffered penalties if he had not carried out the orders of his own Parliament. He was an enemy of England and not a traitor. It was submitted that when France and England were under one sovereign and war broke out between them many men naturalized in the other country fought on the side of their own country of origin and were not put to death when taken prisoner. On p. 1162 of the report it is said: "Mr Heron spoke cursorily and elegantly, but not very materially; Mr Parsons, a young man, spoke boldly and to good purpose; Mr Chute, the civilian spoke learnedly and Mr Hale elaborately and at length" but to no avail, as on 6th March the judges rejected all the pleas of the defence and found the Duke guilty of treason.

About the time the Duke of Hamilton invaded England with the Scots army other risings on behalf of the King were made in Hertfordshire, Essex, Kent and Surrey under the Earl of Norwich, Lord Capel, Sir Charles Lucas, the Earl of Holland and others. The Earl of Holland was taken prisoner at St Neot's and Lord Capel and others were besieged at Colchester where they suffered great hardships. All these uprisings were crushed and led to a series of trials. Burnet says that Hale was counsel for the Earl of Holland and Lord Capel but there is no mention of him appearing in 4 State Trials 1195. Similarly there is no evidence in the reports that he appeared for Lord Craven, although Burnet says the Attorney-General threatened Hale for appearing against the Government to which Hale is said to have answered that: "He was pleading in defence of those laws, which they declared they would maintain and preserve, and he was doing his duty to his client so that he was not to be daunted with threatenings." What is certain is that Hale was no respecter of persons, especially those in high places, as appears from time to time throughout his life.

In 1650 Hale appeared with Mr Maynard and Mr Wild as counsel for the liverymen of the City Companies in a dispute between them and the freemen of London about the election of Lord Mayor and sheriffs. Argument took place at the Guildhall before the Lord Mayor, Court of Aldermen and Common Council and the freemen of London were represented by Major John Wildman and Mr John Price.[9] There appears to have been two petitions, one by the liverymen of the City Companies that the right to elect the Lord Mayor and sheriffs had been theirs for 200 years and was now being threatened. The freemen of London cross-petitioned that they had a right to vote on the election of the Lord Mayor and sheriffs.

This case illustrates the conflicts of the times. There was radicalism in the attempt to establish the rights of the freemen to vote on these important questions which affected their lives so intimately. Who was to exercise power in the City for the ensuing twelve months? Major Wildman for the freemen based his claim on Magna Carta, arguing that the liverymen of City Companies were not chosen either by the City or their respective companies and consequently were not truly representative.

On behalf of the City Companies it was said that even if Magna Carta applied, which was not accepted, the Liberties of London were more ancient than Magna Carta, and Hale had no difficulty in finding authority to establish that the custom of election by the liverymen was of very long standing. The livery-men had a very strong case at law but the system clearly required change with the passage of time and the merits lay with the freemen.

Charles II was crowned in Scotland on 1st January 1651, and at this time considerable correspondence was passing between Charles and the English Presbyterians, including one Presbyterian minister, Christopher Love. Love was a fiery and turbulent man, born at Cardiff, and at one period minister at St Lawrence Jewry in the City of London.

Love was arrested and brought to trial on 14th May 1651.[10] The charge was that he with others in 1649, 1650 and 1651 had tried to raise forces against the Government; had declared Charles II King of England without the consent of Parliament; had helped the Scots to invade the Commonwealth; had main-tained correspondence with Charles II, with the Queen his mother, with other Royalists and the Scots. Evidence was given that about a month after the execution of Charles I Love with others often met at taverns in Dowgate and elsewhere to discuss plans for an agreement between Charles II and the Scots. They sought the agreement of the Queen Mother, and Colonel Titus was sent over to the Continent as their emissary. A reply was sent back which was read to the conspirators at Love's house in the City in his presence.

He was also charged with corresponding with the Scots, and letters were produced from the Earl of Argyle asking that £10,000 should be raised to support an expedition of 5,000 men to Eng-land. Love was active in raising subscriptions, not only subscribing himself but encouraging others to give. On 18th December 1650 Love's wife visited Amsterdam in connection with these secret negotiations.

On 25th June 1651 three counsel were assigned by the court to defend Love, namely Matthew Hale, John Archer and Thomas Walter. Archer and Walter had not taken the Covenant and were therefore debarred from pleading. The Lord President (Mr Keble) specifically asked Hale whether he had taken the Covenant and he affirmed that he had. The Solemn League and Covenant was published by Parliament in 1643 with the object of leading up to the union of the Church of England and the Church of Scotland. The two main provisions were the preservation of the reformed religion in the Church of Scotland and the extirpation of popery and prelacy in England. Hale had taken the Covenant as if he had not done so he would not have been permitted to practise at the Bar.

The burden of Love's defence thus fell on Hale, and he asked the court for time as he had only been instructed between 8 and 9 p.m. on Saturday. He said he had spent all Monday on the case and had only seen Love for the first time that morning, Tuesday. He urged most strongly that it was impossible for him to do justice to the case without further time for preparation. The Lord President pressed him at least to open the case but he refused, saying that he had not even seen the charge and the Attorney-General had refused to give him a copy without the leave of the court. He insisted that it would be a waste of the court's time to try and speak without a copy of the charge as he might deal with points not included in the charge. The Lord President asked Hale whether he had ever known of a prisoner being supplied with a copy of the charge merely because he asked for it. Hale replied that he had often heard of a copy being supplied and knew to his own knowledge that copies had been supplied to Archbishop Laud and the Earl of Strafford.

Hale was compelled to start without a copy of the charge and so played for time. He submitted that in accordance with the Act of 17th July 1649 the words used were "maliciously and advisedly plot" and these words were left out of the charge against Love. He was told by the court that the words used in the charge were "traitorously and maliciously" to which he replied quickly that he would not have put forward the point about the word 'maliciously' if he could have seen the charge. He quoted Coke and raised points of law on all the charges and complained bitterly that he had not seen any of the evidence. He submitted as a matter of law that two witnesses were necessary on a trial for treason, and argued tenaciously throughout the trial. It was all to no avail as on 5th July 1651 Love was convicted and was executed on 22nd August. Hale was by this time in his early forties. It is clear from the report that he had a greater knowledge of the law than the members of the court or the Attorney-General and as an advocate was pertinacious in putting forward every possible point in favour of his client.

The admission book of Lincoln's Inn gives some indication of Hale's progress at the bar. On 18th May 1625 he was admitted to a part of a chambers formerly belonging to Mr Thomas Davey, in the Garden Court on the third floor of the third staircase, on payment of 53s. 4d. Four years later on 2nd July 1633 he moved to better chambers in Garden Court on the first floor of the first staircase. On 12th May 1642 he was appointed a member of a committee to consider Mr Newton's new building. On the 19th June 1643 he was asked to attend the next meeting of the council on the question of keeping commons. It looks as if at the time he was not living in London and was being called to account. However, this does not seem to have affected his standing at the bar, as on 16th November 1648 he was elected a Bencher of Lincoln's Inn.

It is very difficult to find any firm evidence of Hale's private life during this period. It is known that he married Anne Moore, daughter of Sir Henry Moore Bt of Fawley in Berkshire, but the date and place of marriage cannot be traced. The marriage would probably have taken place at Fawley but the records for this period have been destroyed. The marriage probably took place about 1642, as it is believed that the eldest son Robert was born about 1643. It is known that Hale was acquainted with Geoffrey Palmer, later knighted and Attorney-General to Charles II. Palmer's wife was Margaret Moore, daughter of Sir Francis Moore, who was an aunt of Anne Hale, and it may well be that he met his wife at the house of her aunt Margaret.

The Moores were strong Royalists who lived at South Fawley Manor House, Berkshire, built by Sir Francis Moore in 1614. Sir Francis was the author of *Moore's Reports* from 1512–1621, which were subsequently edited by his son-in-law, Geoffrey Palmer. Lord Bernard Sturt and his troop of Life Guards were stationed at Little Fawley in 1644, and he remembered that the arms of Moore with *"Regi et Legi"* were painted over the porch of the Manor House.[11] In 1655 the Commonwealth Government acted against Sir Henry Moore "who was engaged in the last insurrection for cutting down timber at Lorking Farm on his estate".[12] There is some evidence that Hale kept in touch with his wife's family and acted as trustee for his brother-in-law, Sir Seymour Pile, Bt.[13]

Without evidence of the place of birth of the children it is difficult to say with certainty where Hale was living during the Civil War, and it may be that he lived in Oxford for part of the time. There is a tradition that he lived at Greyfriars House, Paradise Street, Oxford, and the house certainly dates from the early seventeenth century.[14] Sir Geoffrey Palmer was in Oxford during the seige of 1646, and Burnet reports that Hale negotiated with Fairfax to preserve the buildings of Oxford. There is a presumption that he must have been at Oxford to carry on these negotiations.

The other possibility is that his home was at Rangeworthy Court near Bristol. Hale's grandfather, Robert Hale, was Lord of the Manor of Rangeworthy and is said to have lived at Rangeworthy Court towards the end of the sixteenth century.[15] The house remained in the family throughout Hale's lifetime, and in

c

1674 he settled the manor of Rangeworthy on his grandson, Matthew.[16] At the time Hale's will was drawn in February 1675 the house had until recently been tenanted by one John Prigge. This house dates from the fourteenth century but the porch bears a date 1664 which indicates that great improvements were carried out by Hale after the Restoration. The house was modernized by Hale, who took off the early roof and built a third storey of seven large rooms and three attics with oak stairways leading thereto and a steeply pitched roof with handsome chimneys. There were corridors in the upper storeys replacing the old idea of connecting rooms. He built Cotswold drip stone mullioned windows of three or four lights and a porch with a room above.[17]

By 1651 Hale was well established in his profession. He was a bencher of his Inn and in demand to act as counsel for the defence in a number of important cases relating to the liberty of the subject when the Commonwealth was proceeding against the individual. There is no recorded case of his appearing for the prosecution during this period, but he does appear to have been well thought of by the Parliamentarians. Burnet says that he was one of the Parliamentary commissioners appointed to treat with commissioners appointed by the King on the fall of Oxford, and that it was on his advice that the buildings of Oxford were saved when captured by Fairfax. There is no doubt that he would have done all in his power to preserve the college buildings, but the main credit must be given to Fairfax, who put a guard on the Bodleian Library as soon as Oxford was captured. Although all his practice was with Royalists, he had taken the Covenant and was therefore permitted to appear in the courts of the Commonwealth on their behalf. By this means he became well known to Parliamentarians, who had many opportunities of assessing his skill and ability as a lawyer.

NOTES

1 Admission book, Lincoln's Inn.
2 ibid.
3 *The History of the Common Law*, 2nd ed., 1716, p. 61.
4 Peter Stein, *Regulae Juris*, p. 48.
5 I am indebted to Professor S. F. C. Milsom for this information.
6 T. B. Howell (ed.), *Complete Collection of State Trials*, London, 1812 (hereafter referred to as *State Trials*), 4, p. 315.
7 ibid., p. 653.
8 ibid., p. 1155.
9 *London's Liberties*, London, 1652.
10 5 *State Trials*, p. 43.

11 Victoria County History: Berkshire, London, 1924, vol. IV.
12 *Calendar of State Papers (Domestic) 1655–6*, p. 2.
13 A deed dated 2nd July 1675 in the possession of Mr Mathew Hale is an acknowledgment that Mary Pile had received her portion of £1,000 from the trustees Sir Matthew Hale and Sir Seymour Pile charged on Ashford Manor, Wilts.
14 Royal Commission on Historical Monuments, City of Oxford 1939, p. 176.
15 Notes made by the late T. Sherwood Hale.
16 See Hale's will, J. B. Williams, *Memoirs of the Life, Character and Writing of Sir Matthew Hale*, p. 333.
17 I am indebted to the present owners of Rangeworthy Court Mr and Mrs Watson for this information.

III

The Hale Commission 1652

After the death of Charles I there was popular clamour for sweeping changes in the law. On 26th December 1651 the Rump appointed a selection committee to nominate suitable persons to serve on a commission to consider the whole question of law reform.[1] On 17th January 1652 the commission was appointed by the House of Commons "to take into consideration what inconveniences there are in the law, and how the mishchiefs that grew from the delays, changeableness, and irregularities in the proceedings in the law may be prevented, and the speediest way to reform the same".[2] Half the members of the selection committee were serving on the Parliamentary Law Reform committee of the House of Commons.[3] This latter committee had a mandate to examine the legal system as a whole, and the Hale Commission reported to the Parliamentary Law Reform committee, who submitted the draft Bills prepared by the Hale Commission to the House of Commons. The leading members of the Hale Commission were Matthew Hale, William Steele, John Sadler and John Fountain, all lawyers. The other members were Major-General Desborough, Colonel Charles George Cocke, Colonel Matthew Thomlinson, moderate army men; Alderman Foulk, William Methold, John Rushworth, Sir Anthony Ashley Cooper, Sir Henry Blount and Sir William Roberts were moderates; the radicals were represented by Josiah Berners and Samuel Moyer the prominent city Baptists, Major William Packer, Colonel Thomas Blount and Hugh Peters; the remainder of the commission consisted of John Mansell, Thomas Manby and John Sparrow.[4]

The commission first met on Friday, 30th January 1652 with fifteen members present, and Hale was elected chairman.[5] The commission met on Mondays, Wednesdays and Fridays weekly until 23rd July and reports appeared in the newspapers from time to time.[6] Hale took the chair on ten occasions until 20th February, when he was succeeded by William Steele the Recorder of London until 22nd March. Colonel Cocke followed until 21st April, William Sadler until 26th May, and John Fountain for the rest of the time.[7] When he was chairman Hale was present at every meeting but after that his attendances fell off and he attended only twenty-five meetings out of a total of fifty-nine. It must have been very difficult for a busy barrister to attend three times a week for six months meetings which lasted all day. On p. 38 of the minutes it is recorded that the commission provided itself with an hourglass and for the convenience of members who wished to spend the weekend in the country it was decided that Friday meetings should adjourn at 2 p.m. until the following Monday at 10 a.m.

When Hale was in the chair a start was made by ordering the clerks in the Court of Chancery and other courts to bring in details of their duties and fees, and the same was done for the Court of Common Pleas, the Attorney-General, the Solicitor-General and the Advocate of the Commonwealth. Draft bills were prepared by sub-committees or individuals and on the 6th February a sub-committee was instructed to prepare a Bill abolishing fines upon bills, declarations and original writs.[8] On 9th February Mr Manby was instructed to draft a Bill on marriage with all convenient speed.[9] It is interesting to note that these two Bills were in fact passed into law. The probable reason is that they were uncontroversial, as everyone wished to reduce the cost of litigation and a proper system of registration of civil marriage was clearly required. On 18th February a suggestion was made that the sheriff should execute all writs which would mean the abolition of all liberties and special jurisdictions, a subject upon which Hale felt strongly. While Hale was in the chair information was obtained about the working of the courts, the procedure of the courts scrutinized, and two Bills were drafted which subsequently became law.

Hale was absent from the committee after 20th February until 5th March, and on Friday 19th March there was a full discussion on the procedure for proving wills and obtaining probate. Fountain, Hale and Manby were deputed to draw up a draft Bill incorporating the resolutions of the committee with power to make such additions as they thought fit and to present the draft Bill to the committee on the following Monday.[10] As Hale would not work on Sunday the time allowed was not over generous, and the minutes on the next Monday make no mention of such a Bill being submitted to the committee. The Bill subsequently drafted bears all the signs of having been prepared by Hale.[11] Jurisdiction in probate is firmly planted in the Court of Common Pleas and provides for the establishment of a probate registry. It sets out clearly the procedure to obtain a grant of probate, prescribes a table of persons entitled on an intestacy and formulates a complete code for the administration of estates. At the end of his administration the personal representative brings his account to the court and obtains his discharge from the court, a method adopted in Scotland today but not in England. Everyone dying within the County of Middlesex or abroad is within the jurisdiction of the Court of Common Pleas, and those dying in other counties are within the jurisdiction of the County Judicatures which it is proposed should be established by another Act. This also corresponds to the Scottish practice today, where probate is dealt with by the local territorial courts, the Sheriff's courts. Hale as a common lawyer supported the proposal to take away probate jurisdiction from the civil law and bring it under the control of the common law.

One of the most controversial Bills was the establishment of County Judicatures. It is important to distinguish between this new court and the old County Courts which it was proposed to abolish. A strong local court based on the county staffed by elected laymen was the key point of Leveller law reform policy.[12] In the commission John Rushworth said, "the management of this affair will render our endeavours either good or bad to the people".[13] It has been suggested that this Bill was drawn up and put forward to the commission for political reasons by the Parliamentary Law Committee.[14] This contrasts with most of the other Bills which came from the commission itself and were approved by the Parliamentary Law Committee. The Bill provided that in every county except London and Middlesex a Court of Record should be established with the same jurisdiction as the courts at Westminster to deal with civil actions. There were to be six judges, one a professional judge from the courts in Westminster, and five elected laymen, one of whom must be learned in the law. These men were to act as judges of the court for a period of three years. The court was to hear all actions by default in their jurisdiction, all personal actions or actions for possession (when no title to land comes in question) and everything which a Justice of the Peace could then do at Quarter Sessions. The court also had jurisdiction to deal with disputes relating to marriage and maintenance, all questions of the validity of marriage to be tried by jury.[15] Full details are set out in the Bill regarding the procedure and the emphasis is on brevity, speed and cheapness. On 31st March Hale made a speech in the commission against a strong County Judicature.[16] He did not approve of laymen on the bench and thought that the place for the layman was on the jury. He was convinced that a judge must be learned in the law and that all important disputes should be heard by the judges of the established courts at Westminster.

The commission proposed to set up a Small Claims Court for the speedy and easy recovery of debts and damages not exceeding the sum of £4.[17] Jurisdiction is based on the petty sessional division of the county and the Justices of the Peace are to appoint five honest and understanding persons to be commissioners to hear and determine differences between party and party living in the same county relating to debt, contract, trespass or detinue of £4 or under. They were to sit weekly at some fixed place to hear the cases put to them. They were to have power by warrant to summons the parties and also witnesses to appear before them and be examined upon oath. Costs are limited to 10s. for the plaintiff and 40s. for the defendant but are not to be included in the £4. Judgment creditors were to have power to distrain on the goods of the judged debtors and sell them. If the goods were not sufficient to meet the debts, the debtor had to work for the creditor until the debt was paid off. One half of the man's wages went to the creditor and the other half for the support of the debtor and his family. If the debtor neglected his work or deserted he could be sent to the workhouse for a month. No attorney was permitted to appear and plead before the commissioners.

The procedure of the Court of Chancery naturally attracted the attention of the reformers, and many of the proposals contained in the draft Bill were sensible and an improvement on the procedure prevailing at the time.[18] The court was to sit in one fixed place and there was to be a chief clerk with as many underclerks as the judges may decide and all fees must be paid to the chief clerk. The process was to be by way of summons and the plaintiff was entitled to insert the names of all the defendants in one summons. If the defendant failed to answer in eight days after appearance the cause could be set down for hearing by default. Copies of the pleadings were to be delivered to the other parties free of charge and there were penalties for not appearing or not filing pleadings. The action was to be heard within fourteen days after close of pleadings and, if this happened during vacation, during the first week of the next term.

A general tightening up of the Masters in Chancery was envisaged. There were to be six Masters appointed by Parliament for a three-year term and there were to be no references to a particular Master. Three were to sit daily in some fixed place attended by the registrar. They were to sit from day to day until the particular question was disposed of and not to adjourn to another fixed date.

The registrar was to keep two books, one for the judges and the other for the Masters. Any motion regarding pleadings was to be heard by the Masters. Cases were to be heard in the order of setting down and an appeal from the report of the Master was to be entered in the judges register to be heard by the judge.

Judges were to sit during the vacation to dispose of all cases not heard at the end of term. They were instructed to give judgment at the time of the hearing and not to reserve judgment save in cases of great difficulty.[19] No more money was to be paid into court unless by the consent of both parties and there was to be no fee for the payment out of money in court.[20] The time for redemption of mortgages in a foreclosure action was not to exceed two years.

It is clear from this Bill that the matter which really troubled litigants at that time was delay. By having the Masters together in one place instead of in offices scattered around Chancery Lane and by making them sit until a decision was reached it was hoped to speed up that part of Chancery litigation dealt with by the Masters. Judgment by default, where a defendant does not appear and put in a defence, was introduced in an attempt to speed up cases where there was no defence, and the idea of giving judgment immediately at the end of the hearing was not adopted in England until the latter half of the eighteenth century and is still not adopted in Scotland or countries where the civil law applies. It is a great saving of time and expense if the parties do not have to come back on a later occasion to hear a reserved judgment.

The Bill, however, never went to the root cause of delay, which was the system of taking evidence on commission by way of interrogatories. It was this system which piled up the costs of copying and bogged down the truth in reams of paper. This system was not questioned by the reformers and detailed directions with regard to the taking and filing of such evidence is set out in the draft Bill.

Not only did the commission consider courts of first instance but put forward proposals for a Court of Appeal. The only method of appeal available at common law was by way of the writ of error. There was no question of a rehearing, but a writ of error was available at the discretion of the court when an error in the record could be alleged.[21] In Chancery the Bill of Review was used to gain a rehearing. There was no system of appeal at common law in the modern sense. The writ of error was frequently used as a delaying tactic, and it was on this ground that it was attacked by the Levellers. In Chancery the Bill of Review could also be used for the purposes of delay and the commission recommended the abolition of both the Bill of Review and the writ of error. The common law conception was that a complaint against judgment must be against the judge. The commission considered the proposal that the Court of Appeal should be given power to penalize the judges for wrong decisions but decided after hard debate that an appeal could be made against a judgment without accusing the judge of misconduct.[22] Even in the later days of the commission on 28th June the question could still be asked, "Why should not judges pay if error in judgment?"[23] Having abolished the only known methods of appeal it was essential for the commission to substitute proposals of its own. It was proposed that a Court of Appeal be established and that all the judges of Chancery, Upper Bench and Common Pleas be eligible for appointment for a three-year term and receive a salary from the Commonwealth. Once every year twenty persons should be appointed by Parliament (none to be lawyers) residing near London and they shall be judges of appeal until re-elected. Notice of appeal must be put in writing and delivered to the Registrar of the Court of Chancery and set down by the Registrar in his book with time of entry. The Registrar was to deliver a copy of the notice to the judge from whom the appeal comes and the other party or his attorney. If the judge would not change the order made by him the appellant must deposit £10 with the Registrar unless he was admitted to sue as a poor man when he paid nothing. The Registrar convened the court, which he did by inviting to sit one judge from each of the courts at Westminster but not from the court from which the appeal lay. He then balloted for seven names from the twenty laymen. Nine judges or any five of them might hear an appeal and their decision should be final.[24]

We do not know what Hale's views were on these proposals but he would clearly be against laymen sitting as members of the court. An interesting feature in the proposal is that the judge of the lower court is invited to reconsider his judgment before the court of appeal is convened to hear the appeal. The method of setting down an appeal is that used today. Notice of appeal is given to the Registrar of the Chancery Division, who enters the notice in a book with the time of entry, and when the appeal comes on for hearing the Daily Cause list gives the date the appeal was set down. Notice of appeal has to be given within a specified time and the appeal is by way of rehearing.

The proposals have a modern ring about them with salaried judges rehearing the case and in some ways are in advance of our present practice. The appeal was to be final and there was no further appeal to the House of Lords or any other tribunal. There was legal aid for the poor, but if a poor man's appeal was rejected he risked being sent to a workhouse for a month and a whipping.[25]

From the 12th May to 4th June the commission considered the question of county registries.[26] It is important to bear in mind that these registries were not intended to deal with land only. There were to be public registries in every county in England and Wales to act as registries of probate and wills and also to be the administrative centre for the County Judicature. They were to be registries for the registration of documents concerning land, judgments, bills of exchange, assignments of debts and powers of attorney. So far as land was concerned it was to be a registry of deeds and not a land registry in the modern sense, where the title is recorded and authenticated by the State.

On Wednesday, 12th May the commission agreed that all mortgages, judgments, rent charges and mesne interests in land should be registered. The Bill eventually drafted provided that no incumbrances against land should be effective against a purchaser for value unless it was registered within twelve months of setting up the registry.[27] All incumbrances created after the establishment of the registry had to be registered in forty days. Provision was made for the registration of documents in the county in which the document is executed and the registrar must send a certificate of lodgment to the registry of the county in which the land lies.

There were grave practical difficulties in these proposals. A man executing a document in London relating to the purchase of land in Northumberland would have to search at the registry in Newcastle before completing his purchase. In a time when communications were bad this would be a formidable task. It is not known what Hale's views on land registration were in 1652, but after the Restoration he wrote against registration on account of all the difficulties and there is no reason to suppose that he changed his mind in the meantime.

Public opinion during the Commonwealth was in favour of some mitigation of the severity of the penalties imposed by the criminal law, and the Bill prepared by the commission on the criminal law is chiefly concerned with abolishing abuses and reducing penalties.[28] The public was disgusted at the spectacle of hardened criminals escaping justice by reason of some technical fault in the indictment while a petty pilferer would be hanged. By modern standards the reduction in punishments were minimal. The punishment of pressing, known as *peine forte et dure*, was abolished; persons convicted of manslaughter should die but their goods should not be forfeited; women should no longer be burnt but drawn upon a hurdle to the place of execution and then hanged;

judgment for the first offence of stealing a horse or picking a pocket should not be death but burning on the left hand, hard labour in chains in a workhouse for two years, whipping once a month, and payment of damages to the injured person; goods of suicides should no longer be forfeited; benefit of clergy was abolished; persons convicted of perjury should stand in the pillory, have both ears cut off, have their nostrils slit and seared with hot irons, suffer six months imprisonment in the workhouse and pay a penalty of three times the damage to the injured person.

On 23rd April the minutes of the Hale commission state: "If he [the accused] will say nothing but stand mute and refuse to plead it shall be taken as a confession and judgment shall follow as if he had confessed it."[29] A clause to this effect was incorporated in the draft Bill. At the present time the astute criminal refuses to make any statement to the police in the hope that the prosecution will be unable to prove its case. It often happens that this is so and the criminal escapes conviction and punishment. Modern thinking is returning to the ideas set out on 23rd April 1652 and questioning why the law should not make the same assumptions as people do in their private affairs. If in the ordinary affairs of life a man is accused of certain conduct and refuses to say anything the assumption is that the accusation is true. If he has some good explanation to give why does he not give it? Why should not the same rules apply in a criminal trial? Hale was not present at the committee on 23rd April, but it is certain that he would have approved as he frequently asserted the importance of the guilty being convicted and punished.[30]

Regulating the fees of the legal profession was high up on the commission's priorities. These were laid down in detail and anyone who charged more would be fined. Counsel's fee on a motion, trial, hearing in chambers or an opinion was fixed at 10s. and argument upon a special verdict or demurrer £1. It was unlawful to give or receive more than the prescribed fee and only a serjeant or a barrister could accept a fee for pleading.[31] All officials were to be paid by fee, fees were prescribed for officials and attorneys, and no attorney was to receive more than 10s. in any one case above the fees allowed. No barrister should take more than £5 in any one case, but nevertheless he must act as counsel for his client until the case was finished.[32] No office can be bought or sold or any premiums given and the penalty is double the sum given.[33] It was an offence for any judge to accept a bribe or for anyone to offer him a bribe. Similarly no office holder should accept more than his just fee.[34]

The system of counsel having fixed fees has been adopted in

Scotland but not in England and it would be interesting to know how many of the ideas put forward during the Commonwealth originated in Scotland. The emphasis of the reform was all on not overcharging either by counsel, attorneys or officials, but, as with Chancery procedure, the real evil of the system was not even diagnosed. Nobody questioned the practice of payment by fees or suggested that judges and officials should be paid a salary except in the case of the proposed Court of Appeal. With a system of payment by fees the difficulties of reform were almost insuperable. Each official had a vested interest in the existing system; the more pleadings, affidavits and appointments there were the more he received in payment. He would surely judge his success by the income he received from his appointment, while justice requires the minimum of paper and appointments.

The reforms of the interregnum can be classified under three main headings: 1. Judicial administration. 2. Humanizing the criminal law. 3. Abolishing known abuses.

1. *Judicial Administration*. The main efforts of the Hale Commission were directed towards a better structure of courts and simplifying procedure in those courts. It was proposed to abolish the Palatine Courts of Durham, Lancaster, Ely and Chester and also courts of quarter session, county courts, sheriff's turns, hundred courts and all other courts of particular liberties and franchises. Hale himself approved of the abolition of the courts of particular liberties.[35] It is doubtful whether he approved the abolition of the Palatine Courts and he certainly wished to retain the county courts for small claims under £10.[36] It was proposed that there should be a Court of Appeal, the Courts of Upper Bench and Common Pleas in Westminster, Courts of County Judicature in each county, petty sessional courts and small claims courts in each division of the county. A number of special courts were retained, including the Court of Admiralty. It was an attempt to establish courts on a regional basis bringing in a lay element in the higher courts in the country.

On the procedural side there was to be judgment by default in civil cases and the accused was to be convicted if he refused to plead. Rules were laid down to tighten up the procedure in the Court of Chancery and reduce delays, while the Court of Common Pleas was to be open all the year round for the issuing of writs and filing of process.[37] Stress was laid on a fixed scale of fees and there were to be penalties for overcharging by officials, barristers and attorneys. Concern was felt about the standards and training of attorneys. The names of all attorneys in the Courts of Upper Bench and Common Pleas were to be written on the rolls of the

Chief Clerk in each court and certified to the Clerk of the Peace of the county where they lived. They were to be presented to a grand jury of the county where they lived to approve those thought fit to continue as attorneys. None were to be eligible to act as attorneys unless they had been educated in one of the Inns of Chancery.[38]

2. *Humanizing the criminal law*. By modern standards this was pitifully small. Some punishments were made less terrible but there was no radical thinking on the subject of punishments. The idea of restitution to the injured persons was introduced, and for stealing a horse not only was a man to be punished but he also had to pay to the owner three times the value of the animal.

3. *Abolition of specific abuses*. This is of special interest as indicating those particular abuses which were troubling men in the mid-seventeenth century. Abolishing fines upon writs and process in the Court of Common Pleas was an obvious example. No fines were payable in the Court of Upper Bench and naturally business flowed to that court. Hale was particularly anxious to get rid of these fines as he wished to retain the Court of Common Pleas and restore it to its proper purpose, the main court to deal with civil actions. Any remaining feudal homage was to be abolished; the lord was forbidden to take a fine from his tenant on a change of tenancy; challenges and duels were to be forbidden; debts were to be assignable; an assignee of a landlord to be able to sue for rent; entails could be barred; transfers of property to wife and children to defraud creditors were forbidden; no office was to be bought or sold; no judges or officials were to be bribed; one type of execution was to cover all chattels, debts, land and all effects except wearing apparel.

There was clearly a great demand by creditors to stop up loopholes whereby debtors could avoid payment and for a simpler system for the execution of judgments.

The reforms proposed during the Commonwealth were on the whole reasonable and modest but they contained a considerable element of bureaucracy and paternalism which seems to be the hallmark of progress. The proposed registries in each county had much to commend them, but the proposal that all deeds, bills of exchange, judgments and other documents should be registered failed to comprehend the formidable practical difficulties. The fees of counsel, attorneys and court officials were fixed by law and there were to be heavy penalties for any infringements. The sale of offices was forbidden but the office-holder remained a freeholder dependant on his fees for a livelihood. Bribery of judges and officials was forbidden. Strict enforcement of the laws against drunkenness, profane cursing and swearing and Sabbath breaking was to be the order of the day. Offenders were to be fined, or, in default of payment, put in the stocks for twelve hours or set to work in the workhouse for a period not exceeding twelve days.[39]

The really radical proposal was the establishment of a Court of Judicature on a regional basis. This did not come from the commission itself but was proposed by the Parliamentary Law Committee and the details were worked out by the commission.

On 20th and 21st January 1653 Parliament spent two days reading "the Book containing the whole system of law" compiled by the Hale Commission, but none of the proposals became law during the lifetime of the Rump.[40] The Nominated Parliament which succeeded the Rump was more active in law reform and on 12th July 1653 ordered the several drafts of Acts prepared by the Hale Commission to be printed for the use of its members.[41] Two of the commissions draft Bills were adopted by the Nominated Parliament. Early in August an Act was passed for taking away fines upon Bills, declarations and original writs and also an act prescribing civil marriage and the procedure to be followed.[42] Both of these Bills were drafted during the first months of the commission when Hale was chairman, and it can be concluded that what he considered to be of the greatest practical importance was approved by Parliament and put into effect whilst none of the other draft Bills reached the Statute Book. Hale himself was probably undisturbed that so little resulted from the hard work put in by the commission as he did not think that the time was propitious for law reform but that such work was best done in a long period of peace.

NOTES

1 Commons Journals VII, 58.
2 ibid.
3 Mary Cottrell, "The Hale Commission of 1652," *The English Historical Review*, October 1968, vol. LXXXIII, p. 690.
4 For a full discussion of the membership of the commission see Mary Cottrell's article *supra*.
5 The minutes of this commission are in the British Museum. Hardwick Papers Add. MS. 35,863.
6 G. B. Nourse, "Law Reform under the Commonwealth and Protectorate," *Law Quarterly Review*, October 1959, vol. LXXXV, p. 518.
7 Minutes *supra*.
8 ibid., p. 15.
9 ibid., p. 17.

10   ibid., p. 70.
11   J. S. Somers, *Collection of Tracts,* vol. VI, p. 196.
12   Mary Cottrell *supra*, p. 697.
13   Minutes *supra*, p. 96.
14   Mary Cottrell *supra*, p. 698.
15   Somers, *Tracts*, vol. VI, p. 211.
16   Minutes *supra*, p. 93.
17   Somers, *Tracts*, vol. VI, p. 184.
18   ibid., p. 202.
19   ibid., p. 207.
20   ibid., p. 209.
21   William S. Holdsworth, *A History of English Law*, vol. I, p. 214.
22   Minutes *supra*, pp. 106–7, 121–3.
23   ibid., p. 172.
24   Somers, *Tracts*, vol. VI, p. 240.
25   ibid., p. 243.
26   Minutes *supra*, pp. 136–55.
27   Somers, *Tracts*, vol. VI, p. 191.
28   ibid., p. 234.
29   Minutes *supra*, p. 124.
30   Hale, *The History of the Pleas of the Crown*, 1st ed., vol. II, p. 193.
31   Somers, *Tracts*, vol. VI, p. 184.
32   ibid., p. 184.
33   ibid., p. 186.
34   ibid., p. 189.
35   Atkins *v*. Clare, Ventris Reports I, p. 399.
36   Francis Hargrave, *A Collection of Tracts Relating to the Law of England*, vol. I, p. 2.
37   Somers, *Tracts*, vol. VI, p. 213.
38   ibid., p. 230.
39   ibid., p. 190.
40   G. B. Nourse, op. cit. p. 522.
41   ibid., p. 522.
42   ibid., p. 523.

IV

Judge of the Common Pleas
1653-7

Cromwell had a great knowledge of men and, knowing Hale's standing at the bar and his work on law reform, wanted to make him a judge. Hale had great scruples about accepting an appointment from Cromwell but was urged to accept by Royalist lawyers such as Sir Orlando Bridgeman and Sir Geoffrey Palmer. Runnington says that Hale at first declined to accept the commission of a judge saying, "that he was not satisfied about his [Cromwell's] authority and therefore scrupled to accept the commission". Cromwell replied, "that as he had gotten possession of the government he was resolved to maintain it. I will not be argued out of it—it is my desire to rule according to the law of the land for which purpose I have pitched on you but if you won't let me govern by red gowns I am resolved to govern by red coats."[1] There was no doubt that Cromwell had the power of government which he intended to wield and Hale's friends urged him to accept.

On 25th January 1653 Hale was appointed a serjeant-at-law preliminary to becoming a judge, and on 30th January 1653 he was appointed a justice of the Court of Common Pleas.[2] He began by going on circuit, dealing with both criminal and civil work. A trial at Lincoln concerned the murder of a townsman who was a Royalist by a soldier of the garrison. The townsman was seen by the soldier with a fowling piece on his shoulder and the soldier told him it was against the laws of the Commonwealth for a Royalist to carry arms. The soldier tried to disarm him but the townsman successfully threw him off. The soldier returned to his unit and told a friend how he had been treated. The two soldiers then went out to search for the townsman and, having found him, demanded his gun. The townsman refused, there was a struggle and the second soldier ran the townsman through with his sword

Sir Matthew Hale, engraved in 1735 from an original painting in
Guildhall, London

Matthew Hale's father, Robert

and killed him. It was at the time of the Assizes and both soldiers were tried. The first soldier was found guilty of manslaughter only and burnt on the hand, whilst the other was found guilty of murder. Colonel Whalley, the commander of the garrison, came to give evidence, saying that the soldier was only doing his duty, and the townsman was killed for disobeying the laws of the land. Hale was not influenced by these arguments, which were bad in law, and sentenced the soldier to death. Up to this point Hale had acted with perfect propriety, but Burnet says he then ordered the sentence to be carried out immediately. He is said to have done this to forestall the possibility of a reprieve which Cromwell would undoubtedly have granted. If so this was a gross impropriety to usurp the functions of the executive and it is doubtful whether it can be accepted as authentic. Hale was a new judge who would naturally be careful to keep within his powers, and to act in this manner was not true to character. He was an extremely able lawyer and would know the limits of his own jurisdiction. In *The History of the Pleas of the Crown* he wrote: "Though I do not deny but the supreme King of the world may remit the severity of the punishment, as he did Cain, yea and his substitutes sovereign princes may also defer or remit punishment, or make a commutation of it upon great and weighty circumstances, yet such instances ought to be rare, and upon great occasion."[3] It is possible that he did not regard Cromwell as a sovereign prince or may have lost his usual self control, but both possibilities are unlikely.

On another occasion Cromwell had ordered a jury to be returned for a trial in which he was interested. Hale heard about this and examined the sheriff, who said that he had no personal knowledge as this was a matter which was dealt with by the under-sheriff. The under-sheriff was then examined and admitted that the jury had been returned by the order of Cromwell. Hale referred to the statute which laid down that all juries ought to be returned by the sheriff or his lawful officer and discharged the jury. Burnet says that "he dismissed the jury and would not try the case". It is difficult to believe that he would not have ordered another jury to be empanelled in a proper manner and have proceeded with the case. In any event it is said that Cromwell was angry and told Hale he was "not fit to be a judge", to which he replied that it was "very true".

He was particularly incensed by the behaviour of some Anabaptists who had rushed into a church and violently disturbed the congregation who were receiving the sacrament according to the rites of the Church of England. He said that "it was intolerable

D

for men who pretended so highly for liberty of conscience to go and disturb others especially those who had the encouragement of the law on their side". The Anabaptists at this time had such influence amongst those in authority that the proceedings were were stopped, much to Hale's disgust.

Burnet says that Hale soon came to the conclusion that it would be better if he concentrated on civil work and did not take criminal cases or cases in which the Government was concerned and that he declared he would "meddle no more with the trials on the crown side". This is almost certainly untrue.[4]

From these remarks by Burnet it would appear that Hale was not popular with Cromwell, but there is other evidence which goes to show that he was held in high repute. Colonel Edward Whalley, said to be garrison commander at Lincoln when the affray occurred between soldiers and townspeople, was in 1656 the Major-General in charge of five Midland Counties. Writing to Oliver Cromwell from Warwick on 31st March 1656 he said: "After the Assizes at Warwick be over which is the last of Judge Hale's circuit . . . I cannot but inform you that Judge Hale hath so demeaned himself in the counties under my charge, both in reference to your highness' interest, as also for his justice to all, and in a special manner taking care of poor men in their causes, without which some would have suffered; as that I desire when he shall wait upon your highness, you would be pleased to take notice of it, and if it seems good to you to give him more than ordinary thanks."[5] Again on 9th April 1656 Major-General Whalley writing to Thurloe said: "I am persuaded that never was any judge on this circuit got more applause, more of the affection of honest men than Judge Hale who as he is unquestionably able, so upon good grounds I judge him a godly man. . . . The judge hath not been free to execute any for horse stealing, but has reprieved them and two others for robbery. He hath interned divers other notorious wicked fellows in the gaol in order to be sent out of the nation."[6] This letter is of interest as it shows that certain offenders were being transported instead of being hanged, but it is not clear whether this was done on the instructions of Major-General Whalley or on the judge's own initiative. What is certain is that he was dealing with criminal business on Assize in 1656 and it is likely that reprieves were being ordered by Whalley. Business at Nottingham was slack, and on 9th August 1656 Whalley was reporting to Thurloe that there had only been twelve trials at the Nottingham Assizes. "I hope every year this will be more and more eased."[7]

Hale was by nature a quick man but schooled himself to listen and be patient. His motto was *"Festina Lente"*, which is one of the adages collected by Erasmus, and there is some support for the proposition that Hale was influenced by the thinking of Erasmus. Erasmus suggested that this proverb should be chased on episcopal rings and engraved on royal sceptres.[8] Hale took the somewhat unusual step of having the proverb engraved on the head of his staff. Erasmus says that if a man in private life does some folly it can soon be repaired, but for a man in authority such as a prince a single hasty decision can raise untold storms.[9] The same thinking appears in Hale's notes on the life of Pomponius Atticus. In his essay on the proverb, *"amortuo tributum exigere"*, Erasmus said: "If you have paid a great deal you may lie and rot in the Church near the High Altar. If you have given stingily, you can be rained on with the common herd outside."[10] Hale gave generously to the Church at Alderley and by virtue of his high office would surely have qualified for a place near the High Altar. Nevertheless he preferred to be rained on outside and gave instructions to that effect.

Hale said that he had "observed many witty men run into great error because they did not give themselves time to think; but the heat of imagination making some notions appear in good colours to them, they without staying till that cooled, were violently led by the impulses it made on them; whereas calm and slow men, who pass for dull in the common estimation, could search for truth, and find it out, as with more deliberation, so with greater certainty". He certainly controlled himself with great strictness and the only indication of inward anger was that his colour would rise a little. Burnet says: "He was always of an equal temper, rather cheerful than merry." He was very patient, always listening with care to everything counsel had to say, thinking that it was better to lose time than patience. In summing up the evidence to a jury he always asked counsel to interrupt him if he had made any mistake of fact.

After he became a judge he made it a practise to pay more for an article than it was worth. He did this to ensure that no vendor should think he had done the judge a favour by selling at a low figure and consequently feel that he had a claim on him. So far as the public was concerned, suspicion might arise of preferential treatment if a judge bought below the market prices. This conduct was not so much the effect of excessive scruples but the measure of his prudence.

When dealing with criminal business he was always careful to bring out any circumstances favourable to the prisoner and not to betray any personal feelings against the prisoner. There was much more examination by the court than there is today, and when he examined a witness he tried to do so quietly so that the witness would not become confused and forget what he had come to say. Pronouncing sentences of death was the part of his work that most went against the grain, but it was a duty which had to be done. He was once pressed to recommend a condemned man for a reprieve, but refused to do so as he did not think he should be pardoned. All he would do was to give a true account of the facts to the Government, whose prerogative it was to grant a reprieve.

He was considerate to the bar, especially the younger and more inexperienced barrister, and if such a man was pitted against very experienced counsel he would try to restore the balance by pointing out matters which might have been overlooked. When giving judgment he always tried by his reasoning to convince all parties of the rightness of the judgment so that they would go away satisfied that the law had been followed and justice done.

Hale was included amongst the list of members who constituted Cromwell's second Parliament on 27th July 1654[11] and the subject of debate was whether the Protector should be elected or hereditary. The majority were against the hereditary principle and Parliament was dissolved without passing any legislation. Thomas Burton records in his diary that it was proposed by Hale that government should be in Parliament and a single person limited and restrained by Parliament and that this appeared to be the general opinion of the House.[12] These views were repeated on 8th February 1658 when Mr Weaver said, "Give me leave to offer Judge Hale's expedient that the single person in possession shall be the single person that shall exercise the supreme magistracy of this nation with such powers limitation and qualifications as the Parliament afterwards shall declare."[13]

In the autumn of 1654 Hale was busy winding up the affairs of John Selden, who died on 16th November, as he was one of the executors of his will with Edward Heyward, John Vaughan and Roland Jewks. John Selden was born in 1584 and was therefore a much older man than Hale. He was a great upholder of the rights and privileges of Parliament and was a member of Parliament for many years. Periods of active politics were interspersed with long periods of study, either in prison or when he retired into private life. Despite his views he was a friend of Clarendon and Laud.

Selden was a man of immense learning and Burnet says that it was through him that Hale was introduced to a wider range of studies than the law. From the evidence of his own books and manuscripts bequeathed to Lincoln's Inn, Hale's scientific interests covered optics, mathematics, including geometry and trigonometry, and medicine. His main interests were, however, philosophy and religion. In youth he had learnt Greek but had apparently forgotten what he had learnt through lack of practice.

Selden had collected a very fine library valued at some thousands of pounds and had formed the intention of giving it to the University of Oxford. In fact, by his will dated 11th June 1653, he left his books to the university. However, he took umbrage against the university when he wanted to borrow a manuscript from the university library and they asked him to enter into a bond for £1,000 for its safe return. Burnet says that he immediately made a codicil to his will striking out the gift to the university, but this is not correct. What he did was to make a deed of gift of all his personal chattels and books to the persons named as his executors, and this deed, dated 27th October 1654, is in the possession of the Bodleian Library. The executors had to decide what to do with the books and, forming the view that Selden really intended his books to go to Oxford University, they gave the library to the university.

Early in 1655 there occurred one of those insurrections against Cromwell by Royalists, and on this occasion it took place in the West Country. Sir Joseph Wagstaff was appointed to command the Royalists and a rendezvous was fixed within two miles of Salisbury. Wagstaff was an intrepid character who had formerly been a Major-General of the foot in the King's army. He was bold in action and reckoned a good fellow but without much intellectual ability. There appeared to be no difficulty in Royalists losing themselves in London, and on the appointed day Wagstaff left London for the West. The King's supporters from Hampshire were late arriving, but Wagstaff met the contingent from Wiltshire at the appointed place. Amongst them was Colonel the Honourable John Penruddock, a man of considerable means and reputation in his own county. Entering Salisbury at five o'clock in the morning they took the city by surprise, locking up all the horses and breaking open the jails. They kept a good body of horse in the market place to control the city and arrested the two judges, Rolle C. J. and Nicholas J., who were on circuit at Salisbury at the time, and the sheriff. Wagstaff resolved to hang the three men forthwith, but many of the county gentlemen, including Penruddock, protested so strongly that he had to give way. Thereafter there was discussion amongst the King's supporters and, without waiting for the men from Hampshire who were in fact on their way, they left for Dorsetshire. The men from Hampshire would not follow and dispersed. Wagstaff and his party continued into Devonshire but, gaining no support, fell into confusion. Some, including Wagstaff, left their horses and went into hiding until such time as they could obtain a ship to the continent. Penruddock and others were taken prisoners by an officer who promised that their lives would be saved.

Cromwell no sooner heard of this than he directed the judges to hold a trial at Exeter. The Chief Justice of the King's Bench at that time was Henry Rolle, who had so narrowly escaped hanging by Wagstaff. He was a man of great learning and experience whose practice throughout had been in the King's Bench. Like Hale he had scruples about serving as a judge under Cromwell. He strongly disapproved of the trial of Charles I and refused to take any part in it. Rolle refused to preside at the trial of Penruddock on the grounds that he might be considered an interested party. Cromwell soon found occasion to replace him by Serjeant Glyn, a man more amenable to directions.

The trial of Penruddock began on 18th April 1655,[14] which was during the vacation, and an express messenger was sent to Hale who was at his country house in Alderley to go to Exeter to take part in the trial. Burnet says: "He refused to go and said 'The four terms and two circuits were enough and that the little interval that was between was little enough for their private affairs,' and so he excused himself; but if he had been urged he would not have been afraid of speaking more plainly." Rigg says that this is unlikely as Penruddock's trial took place at Exeter[15] while Hale belonged to the Midland circuit. On the other hand the story has the ring of truth. The trial took place during the Easter vacation when Hale was at Alderley and the authorities had to produce a court at short notice. There cannot have been many persons qualified to act as judges in the West Country and Gloucestershire is not so very far from Exeter.

A court was very quickly constituted under a commission of assize with Serjeant Glyn and Recorder Steele as judges. Penruddock was not permitted to have counsel to defend him, and Serjeant Glynn conducted the trial in the hectoring manner not uncommon at that time. On 19th April 1655 Penruddock was brought to trial at Exeter on a charge of high treason in levying war against the Lord Protector and the Government and he was convicted and executed on 16th May 1655.

On 1st November 1655 Hale was appointed a member of the Committee on Trade.[16] This committee also included the Chief Justice of the Upper Bench, the Chief Baron of the Exchequer and the Chief Justice of the Common Pleas. The terms of reference of the committee were to regulate and improve trade and to receive propositions for the benefit thereof; to send for customs officers and consult with them; to review all the records of the former Trade Court. The committee first met on 27th November 1655 with power to adjourn from time to time. The committee was set up by Oliver Cromwell as a "Committee and Standing Council for the advancing and regulating the trade and navigation of the Commonwealth".[17] Richard Cromwell was to be president of the committee with a board of forty-five members.[18] The committee, which was provided with a secretary, William Seaman, and two clerks met in the old House of Lords,[19] and as it was large and unwieldy does not appear to have been very effective. The Dutch at first feared that the work of the council would be prejudicial to their trade, but the Dutch ambassador was soon able to write home: "A Committee for Trade was some time since created in England which we then feared would have proved very prejudicial to our State; but we are glad to see that it was only nominal, so that we hope in time those of London will forget that even they were merchants."[20]

Although the committee does not appear to have had much effect it must have proved to have had some value as a similar committee was appointed on 7th November 1660 after the Restoration. The instructions to the 1660 committee were probably based on the experiences of the 1655 committee, particularly as these instructions were largely the work of two of the four members common to Cromwell's committee and the new committee.[21] The 1660 committee was instructed to consider the difficulties of overseas trading; review existing treaties with foreign countries; advise on amendments to existing treaties; suggest new treaties to give greater freedom to merchants; suggest better methods of recovery of debts and execution of judgments, restoration and improvement of manufacturing industry, establishment of standard weights and measures; consider all problems of sea fishing, the balance of trade, whether methods of preference used by foreign countries could not be used by us, problems of money and currency; and to consider the conditions of foreign plantations and giving preference to the imports of the plantations over similar imports from foreign countries.[22]

The committee appears to have been a forerunner of the Board of Trade, and Hale must have learnt a good deal about the problems of trade as a result of his membership of this committee. His interest in trade is shown in his dissertations on the poor and on naturalization, and that he had an extensive knowledge of the condition of trade in his time can be seen in his book on the Customs, written after the Restoration.

Hale continued as a judge of the Court of Common Pleas until the death of Cromwell on 3rd September 1658. He refused to accept the mourning clothes sent to him for the use of himself and his servants and refused to serve as a judge under Richard, despite the fact that he was urged to do so by his brother judges and others. His scruples seem to have reappeared and he said he "could act no longer under such authority". There does not appear to be any difference in principle between serving under Oliver or Richard, but Hale may have thought that as a matter of expediency it might not be wise to serve under Richard. Oliver had the power of the Sovereign but it was by no means certain that Richard could keep that power, and Hale may have foreseen the restoration of the monarchy.

He retired into private life until the Restoration, but was elected as one of the Burgesses for the University of Oxford to serve in Richard's Parliament, which met on 27th January 1658.[28] This was a time which he utilized in study and writing and it is in this period that he wrote his treatise on the poor.

NOTES

1   Charles Runnington, preface to 5th ed., Hale's *The History of the Common Law*.
2   Original appointment in Records Office, Shire Hall, Gloucester.
3   Hale, *The History of the Pleas of the Crown*, p. 14.
4   Thurloe, *State Papers*, vol. 4, p. 686.
5   ibid., p. 663.
6   ibid., p. 686.
7   Thurloe, *State Papers*, vol. 5, p. 296.
8   Margaret Mann Phillips, *Erasmus on his Times*, p. 3.
9   ibid., p. 3.
10   ibid., p. 47.
11   *The Parliamentary History of England from earliest times to 1803*, London, 1817, (hereafter referred to as *Parliamentary History*), vol. IV, p. 1459.
12   Diary of Thomas Burton, vol. I, p. xxxii.
13   ibid., vol. III, p. 142.
14   2 *State Trials*, p. 261.
15   *Dictionary of Natural Biography*: Matthew Hale.
16   *Calendar of State Papers (Domestic), 1655–6*, p. 1.
17   Sir Hubert Llewellyn Smith, *The Board of Trade*, p. 8.
18   Edward Raymond Turner, *Privy Council of England in the 17th and 18th Centuries 1603–1784*, vol. II, p. 316.
19   H. Llewellyn Smith, *The Board of Trade*, p. 9.
20   ibid., p. 9.
21   ibid., p. 11.
22   ibid., p. 251, quoting B. M. Egerton Add MS. no. 2695 f. 268, 269.
23   Anthony Wood, *Athenae Oxoniensis*, vol. II, p. 574.

V

The Poor 1658-9

In the seventeenth century the condition of the poor was particularly unhappy. In the previous century the monasteries had disappeared, the great feudal households had been cut down and many tenants were evicted by enclosures for sheep farming. Others were driven from their land by increased rents, the rise in prices and inflation. The business man of the seventeenth century needed to accumulate capital and to do this it was in his interest to keep down wages, and he felt no responsibility for his workmen in hard times. He appreciated that there had to be some 'poor relief' to prevent the poor becoming desperate, but this was not his personal responsibility. The problem was to force the evicted tenants to work for a wage at some regular employment and consequently indiscriminate charity was frowned on both by Puritans and the employers as it encouraged vagrancy and enabled some men to avoid work. Poor relief had to be associated with hard work and a means test.

It was one of the principles of Puritanism that every man should have a function which should be expressed in some kind of work and the Puritans believed that the idle poor should be put to work. Christopher Hill says: "The great feudal household with its under-employed menials and hangers-on, had no labour problems; but the small craftsman or farmer offered harder work and less excitment to his prospective employees. He needed a body of ideas which would emphasize the dignity of labour for its own sake; which would be critical at once of the careless and extravagant rich, and of the idle and irresponsible poor. He found both in Puritanism."[1]

Marx spoke of the poor laws as the means by which "the agricultural people, first forcibly expropriated were driven from their homes, turned into vagabonds, and then whipped, branded, tortured by laws grotesquely terrible into the discipline necessary for the wage system".[2] But this was not the prevailing view at the time which is given in the works of William Perkins. "Rogues, beggars, vagabonds . . . commonly are of no civill societé or corporation, nor of any particular Church; and are as rotten legges, and armes, that drop from the body. . . . To wander up and downe from yeare to yeare to this ende, to seek and procure bodily maintenance, is no calling but the life of a beast."[3] That men might have been turned into beasts by reason of their treatment at the hands of other men and be deserving of sympathy does not seem to have occurred to many of their contemporaries.

In Hale's time the statute law on the subject was as follows. The first Act was 43 Elizabeth cap. 2 which enabled the churchwardens and overseers of the poor to do a number of things:

1. To set to work children whose parents were not able to maintain them.
2. To set to work those who had no means of supporting themselves—but no sanctions were given against those who refused to work.
3. To levy a rate on parishioners to raise sufficient money to buy a stock of flax, hemp etc. upon which the poor could work.
4. To provide for those who were unable to work from the rate.
5. To apprentice poor children—but no power to compel any employer to accept them.

The statute 7 James cap. 4 refers to rogues, vagabonds and idle and disorderly persons and enables the Justices of the Peace to send them to a house of correction which they have power to build. The master of the house of correction is given power to keep them at work.

In 1659 Hale wrote *A Discourse Touching Provisions for the Poor*, not published until 1684,[4] in which he pointed out the defects in the law. The Act of James I dealt only with idle and disorderly persons and not with the poor without means of support. There was no provision in that Act for the raising of stock upon which to work, and as the description was very wide it could be abused by the justices.

Hale comments that the Act of Elizabeth had never really worked with regard to the provision of stock because the ratepayers did not want it. In the short term it would have meant increased rates to provide the stock although in the long term it would have been beneficial. Also where the poor were most numerous the ratepayers were usually tradesmen whose policy was always to oppose any rates being imposed on stock and to limit rates to land and houses. As a result the rates levied were small and insufficient for the purpose. The Act gave no power to the justices to compel churchwardens or overseers to raise money for stock if they neglected to do so; the Act applied only to each individual parish, which was in many instances too small a unit; there was no power to erect a common workhouse for several parishes.

Hale proposed a detailed plan for providing work for the poor. The justices at quarter sessions were to combine the parishes into several divisions in each of which there should be a common workhouse for the division, and assess the rate for each parish. The justices should appoint a master for each workhouse at a salary on a three-year contract and two overseers responsible for the issuing and return of the stock and taking the master's accounts quarterly or monthly. At the end of the year the overseers and master must render accounts to the justices, which accounts were to be published and made available for public inspection.

The master and overseers of each workhouse were to be a body corporate capable of receiving gifts or legacies for the benefit of the poor within the parish and accountable to the justices and their successors for the right use of the funds received. They were not, however, to be able to hold land on lease for more than one year.

If a poor person was able to work but refused to do so he might be compelled to work by a warrant of two justices imprisoning him in the workhouse with "moderate correction". The same penalties were awarded to those who stole the stock or deliberately spoilt their work.

Hale says that there would be many benefits to the country if his scheme were put into operation. By incorporation and good administration charitable people would be encouraged to give funds to the workhouses for the benefit of the poor. He urges that this is a constructive charity, and while hospitals provide for those who cannot help themselves, workhouses would enable the poor to establish themselves and make their own living. He forecasts that the wealth of the nation would be increased and sees no reason why England should not improve its standard of living as well as Holland and Flanders and Barbados if only we worked as hard and managed our affairs as well as the men in these countries. He claims that it was not a question of disposition but of training and that the English would be as successful as the Dutch if they were trained to work in the same way as the Dutch. He then goes on to explain that such a scheme would be of benefit to our balance of payments by increasing the goods available for export, so that our exports exceeded our imports. This he claims is the only way to increase our wealth, for if imports exceed exports the excess can only be made good by money sent abroad.

Work done in workhouses would increase the stock of manu-
factured articles such as woollen manufactures (kerzies, serges,
baize) available for export. Some of these manufactures were confined to certain parts of the country, such as Devonshire, Norfolk
and Colchester, and they might be made all over the country.
Certain parts of the country, such as Lincolnshire and Northamptonshire, had little woollen manufactures and Hale envisaged these
counties knitting stockings, caps, waistcoats and the like. He also
foretold an increase in linen manufactures such as linen clothes,
laces of all sorts and sails, and if these could be made at home
foreign currency would be saved and imports from Holland and
France would not be required. He replied to the argument that
we did not have the raw materials by saying that if there was a
demand for these materials farmers would very soon sow hemp
and flax and possibly land which was not suitable for other crops
could be used for these crops. He said that 2 acres of hemp and
flax grown in each parish would employ multitudes, and when it
was known that work was available instructors would come from
foreign lands and their skills would be learnt which would be for
England's benefit. He argues that once a stock of raw material is
purchased very little further capital should be required as sales
would provide the capital needed and the charge on the rates
should become less and less every year.

To objections that it would be costly to the rates to start with
he replies that in the long run it would be an economy as the
burden on the rates in later years would diminish and perhaps
disappear altogether. Some said that there are many people who
would rather beg than work and Hale agrees that there would have
to be a law to compel idlers to work and they would find it more
profitable to work than to beg. He also thinks that children should
be educated to work and in this way there would be fewer idle
persons. If men knew that there was work for the poor to do they
would stop giving to beggars and the latter would find it better
to work than to beg. He accepts the fact that in general men
work better for themselves than they do for a public corporation.
On the other hand there were favourable trading conditions for
a public corporation as well as a private trader and in good times
a profit should be made. In bad times, even though no profit was
made, the workhouse gave the poor a means of subsistence and
the charge on the rates was probably less than it would be without a workhouse. When business was prospering the poor might
leave the workhouse for better-paid jobs in private enterprise, but
there was no objection to this as the only purpose of the workhouse was to provide work when it could not be obtained in the

open market. It would be justified only as a refuge for the poor in times of need when they were unemployed.

Hale summed up by saying that the scheme was a work of great humanity:

> And indeed the ill provision for the poor in England is one of the greatest reproaches to us in relation to our Christian profession.
> A work for a good Englishman. The want of a due provision for education and relief of the poor, in a way of industry, is that which fills the gaols with malefactors and fills the kingdom with idle and unprofitable persons, that consumes the stock of the kingdom without improving it, and will daily increase to desolation in time; and the error in the first concoction is never remediable but by gibbets and whipping. But there must be found a prudent, and resolved method for an industrious education of the poor, and that will give better remedy against these corruptions than the after gain of penalties can.

Here we find Hale well in advance of his times, advocating a public trading corporation intended to make a profit but its main object to provide a living for the poor when they found themselves unemployed by reason of the vagaries of trade.

In his personal life Hale set aside one-tenth of his income for the poor and took care to be informed about those in greatest need. After he became a judge some of his fees were sent anonymously to the prisons to discharge poor prisoners.

When he was at Alderley, if he came across a beggar he would ask whether he was capable of working. If he replied that he could find no work to do he was employed by Hale to gather up all the stones in a field and well paid for the job. Hale would then arrange for one of his carts to collect the stones and used them for road repairs. When Hale was in London he gave to all that asked and was upbraided by his friends for encouraging idleness. He replied that most of them were probably rogues and idlers but there might be some amongst them who were in real need and he would rather give charity to twenty rogues rather than miss one who had need of the small help he could give. This was a personal and independent line to take which would not be favoured by the Puritan thinkers of his time.

Burnet says that he invited his poor neighbours to dine with him and that he did this for the poor of neighbouring parishes as well as his own. If anyone was sick he sent them warm food from his own table. Laslett says: "The literature of the Tudor and Stuart age is full of laments about the decay of housekeeping, which meant amongst so many other things, holding open-house for the tenantry."[5] What Hale was doing was therefore keeping up the old tradition of the good landlord and not embarking on any new practice nor acting in any eccentric way.

A story is told of a poor man who had lost his job on account of his own misbehaviour and came to Hale for a reference. Hale refused and the man fell on his knees begging for his help. Finding that his pleas were of no avail he turned to abuse saying that he would be utterly ruined and would curse Hale for the rest of his days. Hale replied that he could very well bear his abuse but could not give him a reference, and sent him away with a sum of money.

Events now began to move quickly towards the Restoration, and Hale was a member of the Parliament which met on 25th April 1660.[6] He was returned as a knight of the shire for Gloucester but was reluctant to stand. He did not agree until three days before the election and the Earl of Berkeley bore all the costs of the election and acted as his campaign manager, even going to the extent of lending him a sword which protocol required. Burnet adds: "But he was soon weary of it for the embroidery of the belt did not suit well with the plainness of his clothes."

In Parliament Hale moved that a committee might be appointed to look into the proposition that had been made by Charles and the concessions that had been offered by the late King during the war, particularly at the Treaty of Newport, and that Parliament should send over to the King firm propositions in reply. Burnet says that this motion was seconded but he does not say by whom. Colonel Edward King had supported Hale in his opposition to the return of Charles without conditions. According to the fragmentary record of the debate in the Bodleian Library Sir William Morice began by saying, "Mr Speaker there are divers persons that would have the King brought in upon terms, others upon no terms at all. To bring in His Majesty without terms will not be secure for us nor safe for him." He moved the House to draw up a Bill for the King's approval.[7]

Hale and his supporters were opposed by the full weight of Monk, who told the House that there was great danger in delay. Might not they put these propositions to Charles after he had come over? Charles was bringing neither an army nor treasure with him. Monk moved they should immediately send commissioners to bring the King over and that all the blame for any bloodshed or mischief which might arise at home would rest on those who insisted on any motion which might delay the present settlement of the nation. Burnet says: "This was echoed with such a shout over the House that the motion [Hale's] was no more insisted on."

NOTES

1   Christopher Hill, *Puritanism and Revolution*, p. 223.
2   Quoted by Christopher Hill, *op. cit.* p. 224.
3   Quoted by Christopher Hill, *op. cit.* p. 227.
4   Also published in *The Works moral and religious of Sir Matthew Hale*, London 1805, edited by the Rev. T. Thirlwall, vol. I, p. 519.
5   Peter Laslett, *The World We Have Lost*, p. 68.
6   Gilbert Burnet, *History of His Own Time*, vol. II, p. 1160.
7   Clayton Roberts, *The Growth of Responsible Government in Stuart England*, p. 144.

VI

Chief Baron of the Exchequer
1660-64

The Restoration was a time of great rejoicing whilst the King was in a generous mood ready to do justice to all his subjects. He had been assisted greatly in his return by the Presbyterians in the Church of England who had worked for the restoration of the monarchy. He wanted both sides to make concessions and did make sincere efforts to bring about a reconciliation between the orthodox members of the Church of England and the Presbyterians in the Church. The Presbyterians suggested to Archbishop Usher that nothing should be laid down about wearing of surplices, the cross in baptism, and kneeling at the Communion and that it should be left to each man's conscience to do as he thought right. The King asked the Presbyterians to submit proposals in writing about Church government promising them a meeting with representatives of the Church of England in his presence. The Presbyterians met at Sion College to draw up proposals which were ready in about two or three weeks' time, and a paper was submitted to the King. The King was pleased with what he read and said that he was glad that they accepted the episcopacy and the liturgy and had no doubt that terms could be agreed.

The Presbyterians expected that the bishops on their side would also submit proposals, but none were forthcoming. The bishops were in a bitter mood, and this was understandable from a human point of view. They had lived in exile or in disgrace for long years but were now in a strong and entrenched position and were not willing to parley with those who had so recently been their enemies. The bishops made no concessions of any kind, and the Presbyterians were left with the choice of remaining in the Church of England on its own terms or resigning their livings.

The Church party took steps to enforce the old penal laws of Queen Elizabeth and people were fined for not going to church.

A seventeenth-century part of Lincoln's Inn

(*left*) John Selden, engraved from a Bodleian Library painting attributed to Sir Peter Lely

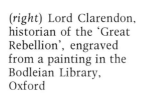

(*right*) Lord Clarendon, historian of the 'Great Rebellion', engraved from a painting in the Bodleian Library, Oxford

Many Presbyterians were suspended and ejected from their livings and a petition was presented to the King by the Presbyterians asking him publicly to declare that he wished all proceedings under the penal laws to cease until a settlement had been reached. The King received a deputation from the Presbyterians sympathetically and said that he would put what he thought fit in a declaration which was delivered to the Presbyterians on the 4th September 1660. A meeting was called for 22nd October, when both sides could put forward any points they might have on the declaration. The declaration was acceptable to most of the Presbyterians, and on the strength of it Dr Reynolds accepted the bishopric of Norwich. Mr Baxter was offered the bishopric of Hereford but refused it on other grounds, while Mr Calummy refused the offer of the bishopric of Lichfield and Coventry until after the declaration had been passed into law.

A Bill was prepared on the lines of the declaration but failed to get a second reading in the House of Commons. Neal says: "Sir Matthew Hale who was very zealous for the declaration was at that very juncture taken out of the House of Commons, and made Chief Baron of the Exchequer, that he might not oppose the resolution of the Ministry."[1] On 8th November 1660 the House thanked the King for his declaration, nobody opposing it, and on 28th November rejected it. The opponents in the Church must have mobilized their forces in the intervening period, but it is certain that Hale had no influence one way or the other as he was appointed Chief Baron on 7th November. Hale was a great supporter of the declaration, and Emlyn says: "He was a great lamenter of the divisions and animosities which raged so fiercely at that time among us, especially about the smaller matters of external ceremonies which he feared might in the end subvert the fundamentals of all religion. Although he thought the non-conformists too narrow he strongly disapproved of the penal laws against them as he knew that many of them were peaceable men who had disliked the Commonwealth. He thought they deserved better treatment; opposed those laws as an infringement of the rights of conscience which he believed to be inviolable; and thought that the only way of healing the breaches was a new Act of Uniformity."[2]

After the rejection by Parliament of the King's declaration the Church party found itself securely in the saddle and the screw was turned tighter and tighter on Dissenters. An Act of Parliament was passed restoring ministers to the livings they had lost under the Commonwealth by 25th December 1660 and requiring the present incumbent to quit. In 1661 the Corporation Act was

E

passed. Nobody who had not taken communion in accordance with the rites of the Church of England during the twelve months prior to election could hold municipal office. In 1662 an Act of Uniformity was passed compelling all ministers, dons and schoolmasters each year to make a declaration assenting to everything prescribed by the Book of Common Prayer. The Conventicle Act became law in 1663, whereby it was made an offence to go to any separate meeting for religious worship where more than five persons were present besides the family.

One of the first acts of the King was to bring twenty-nine regicides to trial, and in May 1660 the judges met at Serjeants Inn to consider the procedure and management of the trial. Hale was not at that time a judge and was not concerned with these preliminaries. He was appointed Serjeant-at-law by the King on 22nd June 1660, although he had previously been appointed a Serjeant by Cromwell.[3] Thirty-seven judges were nominated for the trial, including Serjeant Hale, and the trial itself was held at the Old Bailey from 9th to 16th October 1660.[4] The conduct of the trial was in the hands of Sir Orlando Bridgeman, then Chief Baron of the Exchequer, and there is no record of Hale taking any active part in the trial. It is certain that he would have found this particular trial most distasteful.

On 1st May 1660 Hale was appointed a member of a committee to peruse the journals and records and examine the Acts and orders passed into law during the Commonwealth and to report and advise; also to make suggestions to carry on the Courts of Justice and how former decisions may be made good.[5]

Hale spoke twice in the debate on the Indemnity Bill, once in the House of Commons on 6th July 1660[6] and once in a conference between the Lords and Commons when he moved that the matter be referred to a committee for the full facts to be ascertained. This was agreed.[7]

On 7th November 1660 Hale was appointed Chief Baron of the Court of Exchequer.[8] The Earl of Clarendon, the Lord Chancellor, made a speech when delivering the commission to Hale, saying among other things that if the King could have found out an honester and fitter man for that employment he would not have promoted Hale but he had been preferred as he [the King] knew none that deserved it so well.

It was usual for the Chief Baron to be knighted, but Hale wished to decline and avoided waiting on the King. The Lord Chancellor saw what was happening and invited Hale to his house on business. The King was in the house at the time and Hale was taken to him to be knighted before he had time to demur.

He laid down certain rules to be observed in his conduct as a judge.

Things necessary to be continually had in remembrance
1. That in the administration of justice, I am entrusted for God, the King and Country; and therefore
2. That it be done (1) Uprightly (2) Deliberately (3) Resolutely.
3. That I rest not upon my own understanding or strength, but implore and rest upon the direction and strength of God.
4. That in the execution of justice, I carefully lay aside my own passions, and not give way to them however provoked.
5. That I be wholly intent upon the business I am about, remitting all other cares and thoughts as unseasonable and interruptions.
6. That I suffer not myself to be prepossessed with any judgment at all, till the whole business and both parties be heard.
7. That I never engage myself in the beginning of any cause, but reserve myself unprejudiced till the whole be heard.
8. That in business capital, though my nature prompts me to pity, yet to consider that there is also pity due to the country.
9. That I be not too rigid in matters purely conscientious, where all the harm is diversity of judgment.
10. That I be not biassed with compassion to the poor, or favour to the rich in point of justice.
11. That popular or court applause or distaste, have no influence into any thing I do in point of distribution of justice.
12. Not to be solicitous what men will say or think, so long as I keep myself exactly according to the rule of justice.
13. If in criminals it be a measuring cast, to incline to mercy and acquittal.
14. In criminals that consist merely in words when no more harm ensues, moderation is no injustice.
15. In criminals of blood, if the fact be evident, severity in justice.
16. To abhor all private solicitations of whatever kind soever and by whomsoever in matters depending.
17. To charge my servants (1) Not to interpose in any business whatsoever (2) Not to take more than their known fee (3) Not to give undue preference to causes (4) Not to recommend counsel.
18. To be short and sparing at meals that I may be fitter for business.

There is no mention in these rules that a judge should not interrupt counsel, nor is there anything said about despatch in judicial business. He was extremely thorough in all his work and this gave rise to the only complaint made against him that he did not have sufficient despatch in business. This thoroughness meant that every case was considered from all angles and any suit heard by him was seldom tried again. He was very patient and no consideration of his own convenience would make him hurry the hearing. For this reason he made it a rule, especially on circuit, to have only a short interval for food so that he would be fit to continue the hearing in the afternoon and would have sufficient time for a full consideration of the matter before him.

He was very particular about not reaching a decision until all the evidence had been heard and not giving any indication of his views to the parties before judgment. He concealed his opinions so carefully that the other judges sitting with him could not see which way his mind was moving. Burnet says that his reason was that a judge should come to his own conclusion uninfluenced by the views of his brother judges. It sometimes happened when Hale was Chief Baron that when all the judges had delivered their opinions Hale expressed his opinion with such good reasoning that the other judges changed their views and agreed with him.

There were three of his rules which applied particularly to the time in which he lived. Rule No 11 is that a judge should not be influenced by popular or court applause. In Cromwell's time, as has already been related, he refused to take part in the trial of Penruddock which would not make him popular with Cromwell. In Charles II's time on one occasion when he was on circuit the grand jury presented a respectable Non-conformist for breaches of the penal laws. Hale rebuked them in no uncertain terms telling them to concentrate their attentions on "profaneness, drunkenness, and other immoralities which abound daily amongst you". He said that if they persisted he would transfer the proceedings to London in Westminster Hall. He said that if this did not stop the prosecution he would resign, as he had told the King when he accepted the office of Chief Baron of the Exchequer that if he was pressed to do things against his conscience he would resign. This seems to have effectively stopped the prosecution.

There is no doubt that Hale's sympathies were with the Non-conformists and Quakers, and a letter written on 30th September 1664 states that Newgate was so full of Dissenters that fever was carrying them off. It goes on: "There is great hope from a report of Judge Hale that the proceedings on the Conventicle Act will stop, for at Exeter the Quakers were by this means found not guilty, because no sedition appeared, and the Act is not against religious meetings, but seditious conventicles. The statutes would do little hurt if put into execution by impartial judges."[9] It is clear that Hale used all his judicial ingenuity to combat these Acts. The mere threat of transferring cases to London would be sufficient to stifle most proceedings.

Rule No 16 was to the effect that he would abhor all private solicitations of all kinds. On one occasion a peer went to see Hale about a case in which he was interested to make sure that he knew all the facts before it came into court. Hale interrupted him to say that it was his practice never to receive any information about a case before it came into court so that all parties could be heard alike and refused to hear any more. The Duke, much disgruntled, complained to the King, who told him that he was fortunate to have got off so lightly and that he believed if he [the King] had behaved in a similar way he would have had the same treatment. On another occasion when Hale was on circuit one of the parties to an action at the Assize sent him a buck for his table. When the case came on for hearing he said that the trial could not proceed until he had paid for the buck. The gentleman replied that he never sold his venison and gave a buck to every judge who came on Assize. This was confirmed by others present but Hale persisted and the case was taken out of his list and stood over until the next Assize. In the same way at Salisbury, in accordance with custom, the Dean and Chapter presented him with six sugar loaves, but Hale made his servants pay for the sugar loaves before proceeding with the case. Hale may have been excessively scrupulous, but in a time when standards in these matters were low there is much to be said for his strict adherence to the highest standards.

Rule 17 directed his officials not to intervene between the judge and a suitor. The officials in all the courts had vested interests in the survival of the system and delay in bringing a matter before the judge might well be a denial of justice. They were not to give priority to particular suitors nor were they to recommend counsel, nor to accept bribes.

It is one of the facts of litigation that business flows to a good judge. As Hale had the reputation of being a good judge business was attracted to any court in which he was sitting. Practitioners in many cases had a choice of the court in which to start an action and as a result of Hale's high reputation they would make certain that the hearing took place before him.

NOTES

1 Daniel Neal, *The History of the Puritans*, vol. IV, p. 251.
2 Sollom Emlyn, preface to Hale's *The History of the Pleas of the Crown*, p. v.
3 J. M. Rigg, *Dictionary of National Biography*: Matthew Hale.

4   5 *State Trials*, p. 947.
5   4 *Parliamentary History*, p. 25.
6   ibid., p. 80.
7   ibid., p. 101.
8   *Calendar of State Papers (Domestic) 1660–61*, p. 354.
9   *Calendar of State Papers (Domestic) 1664–65*, p. 20.

VII

Trial of the Witches 1664

At the Assize held before Hale on 10th March 1664 at Bury St Edmunds, Suffolk, Rose Cullender and Amy Duny, widows, both of Lowestoft, were indicted for bewitching Elizabeth and Anne Durent, Jane Bocking, Susan Chandler, William Durent, Elizabeth and Deborah Pacy.[1] Rigg in the *Dictionary of National Biography* refers to Amy Drury and Campbell to Amy Duny. Drury is the spelling used in the report in *6 State Trials* and Duny is the spelling used in a book published in 1683, *A short treatise touching Sheriff's Accompts, together with a report of the trial of the witches at Bury St Edmunds*, said to have been written by Hale's marshal. It is this version which is preferred.

The report on the trial starts dramatically.

Three of the parties above named, viz. Anne Durent, Susan Chandler and Elizabeth Pacy were brought to Bury to the Assizes and were in reasonable good condition; but that morning they came into the Hall to give instructions for the drawing of their bills of indictment, and the three persons fell into strange and violent fits, shrieking out in a most sad manner, so that they could not in any wise give any instructions in the court who were the cause of their distemper. And although they did after some certain space recover out of their fits, yet they were every one of them struck dumb, so that none of them could speak neither at that time, nor during the Assizes until the conviction of the supposed witches.

Dorothy Durent, the mother of William Durent, said in evidence that on or about 10th March she had to go away from home and had nobody to look after her child, William, who was not yet weaned. She asked Amy Duny to look after the baby in her absence and promised her a penny for her services. She gave firm instructions to Amy Duny not to suckle the child. The judge interposed to ask her why she had done this as Amy Duny was too old to suckle a child. Dorothy Durent replied that Amy Duny had for some years past had the reputation of being a witch, and it was for this reason that she gave the caution. Also the report adds: "That it was customary with old women, that if they did look after a suckling child, and nothing would please it but the breast, they did use to please the child to give it the breast, and it did please the child, but it sucked nothing but wind, which did the child hurt." On her return Amy Duny told her that she had suckled the child despite the request not to. Dorothy was angry with her and there was a violent quarrel. Continuing her evidence Dorothy said that that very night William became ill with fits of swooning which continued for several weeks. Dorothy was so concerned about the child's health that she consulted a Dr Jacob of Yarmouth, who had a reputation in this field. He advised her to hang up the child's blanket in the chimney corner all day and that when she came to wrap up the child in the blanket at night she was not to be afraid if she found anything in the blanket but to throw it in the fire. Dorothy did as she was told and when she came to take down the blanket at night a great toad fell out of it which ran up and down the hearth. There was only a youth in the house with Dorothy at the time and he caught it with some tongs and put it in the fire. The report says "as soon as it was in the fire it made a great and horrible noise, and after a space there was a flashing in the fire like gunpowder, making a noise like the discharge of a pistol, and thereupon the toad was no more seen nor heard". The judge enquired whether after the noise and flashing were not the remains of the toad to be seen in the fire, but Dorothy replied that there was nothing to be seen.

Dorothy then continues with some hearsay evidence that the next day a young woman, a relative of Amy's, went to see Amy and told Dorothy that she found Amy badly burned on her face, legs and thighs. Amy blamed Dorothy for her condition and said that she would live to see some of her children dead, and herself on crutches. Dorothy continued that after the burning of the toad William recovered, but that about 6th March her daughter Elizabeth aged about 10 years had similar fits and during her illness complained about Amy. Dorothy went to an apothecary for something for her child and on her return found Amy in the house, and when questioned Amy said that she had come to see the child to give her some water. Dorothy became very angry with Amy and turned her out of the house. Amy in going said, "You need not be so angry for your child will not live long." This was on Saturday. On the following Monday Elizabeth died and Dorothy blamed Amy for the death by her witchcraft. Not long after the child's death Dorothy became lame in both legs and had to use crutches. The judge asked whether at the time of her lameness there had been any stoppage of menstruation but she replied not.

Samuel Pacy gave evidence about his two children, Elizabeth aged 11 years and Deborah Pacy aged 9 years. He was a merchant from Lowestoft and proved a good witness, giving his evidence well without undue emphasis. On Thursday 10th October 1664 his younger daughter Deborah suddenly became lame so that she could not stand and she remained in this condition until 17th October. On that day, as the weather was mild and sunny, she asked to be taken to the eastern side of the house so that she could sit on a bank overlooking the sea. Whilst she was there Amy Duny came to the house to buy some herrings but she was refused and went away in a bad humour. She came back again on two further occasions but received the same reply and went away grumbling. Nobody heard exactly what she said, but at that moment Deborah was taken with violent fits and pain in her stomach "shrieking out in a most dreadful manner like unto a whelp and not like a sensible creature". She continued with these fits until 30th October. The father consulted Dr Feaver but the doctor failed to diagnose the cause of these fits. The father said that the child cried out that Amy Duny was the cause of her illness and was frightened by apparitions of her. He, therefore, charged her with being a witch and had her put in the stocks on 28th October. Examined in the stocks Amy said, "Mr Pacy makes a great stir about his child, but let him stay until he hath done as much by his children as I have done by mine." Being further questioned about what she had done to her children she answered, "That she had been fain to open her child's mouth with a tap to give it victuals." Within two days of Amy saying this the eldest daughter Elizabeth had such a bad fit that they could not open her mouth to feed her without giving her a tap. The same thing happened to Deborah and she had to be given a tap. Both children in their delusions referred to Amy and also Rose Cullender.

The fits were various: sometimes the children would be lame on one side of the body and sometimes on the other; sometimes there was a soreness over their whole bodies so that they could not endure anyone touching them; at other times they could use their limbs but lost their hearing; at other times they lost their sight or speech; on one occasion they lost their speech for eight days. At other times they would fall into a swoon and upon recovering their speech would have violent coughing, bringing up much phlegm and bent pins and a two-penny nail. The father stated that there were forty pins, the two-penny nail had a very broad rim and that he was himself present when some of the pins had been vomited up. A pin would come up after every fit and there were often as many as five fits in a day. The father continued that the children remained in this state for about two months and when, during their intervals of lucidity he got them to read some passages from the New Testament, he observed that they could read until they came to the words Jesus or Christ but as soon as they did so they fell into another fit. But when they came to the name of Satan, or the devil they would clap their hands on the book, crying out, "This bites, but makes me speak right well." The children also said that Amy Duny and Rose Cullender would appear before them, shaking their fists at them and threaten them that if they told what they had seen they would be tormented more than ever. The father was at his wits end to know what to do and eventually decided to send the children to Yarmouth to stay with his sister, Margaret Arnold, in the hope that the change of scene and air would do them good.

Margaret Arnold was the next witness and she said that the children came to her on 30th November. Her brother had explained the position and said he thought that the children were bewitched but she did not believe him. She thought the children had been up to tricks and had put in the pins themselves. She therefore took all the pins out of their clothes and sewed them up instead. She found she was mistaken because the children had vomited at least thirty pins in her presence and had had very violent fits. The children would in their fits cry out against Amy Duny and Rose Cullender, saying that they could see them, and were threatened by them that they would be tormented ten times as much if they said anything. Sometimes only the children would see things running up and down the house looking like mice, and one of them caught one with the tongs and threw it on the fire where it screeched out like a rat. On another occasion Deborah went out of doors to get some fresh air and a bee flew into her face; she rushed back into the house and fell into a fit; after much pain she vomited a two-penny nail with a broad head and when she came out of the fit she told her aunt that the bee had forced the nail into her mouth. Once Elizabeth was sitting by the fire when she started up and said that she saw a mouse, and crept under the table looking for it; at length she put something into her apron saying she had caught it; immediately she ran to the fire and threw it in and there was a flashing like gunpowder, but the aunt saw nothing in the child's hand.

Deborah had complained that Amy had been with her in her fits and had tempted her to drown herself and to cut her throat.

Both children complained in their fits of Amy and Rose saying, "Why do not you come yourselves, but send your imps to torment us?"

With regard to Anne Durent, her father, Edmund Durent, gave evidence that he lived in Lowestoft and that about the end of November Rose Cullender came to his house to buy herrings from his wife. His wife refused to sell her any and she went away very discontented. On 1st December his daughter Anne fell ill with serious stomach pains and swooning fits, and after her recovery said that she had seen Rose, who had threatened to torment her. She vomited pins which were produced to the court. Edmund Durent's evidence was confirmed by one Ann Baldwin.

Jane Bocking was so weak that she could not be brought to the Assizes and evidence was given by her mother, Diana Bocking who also lived in Lowestoft. She said that Jane suffered from swooning fits but had been better of late. Upon the 1st February she had a recurrence of the fits with great pain in her stomach. When her fits were on her she would spread out her arms with her hands open and appear as if she was catching something and would close her hands. When her hands were forced open crooked pins would be found but nobody knew how they got there. On another occasion Jane appeared to be talking to somebody else in the room although there was nobody else there. She would frequently complain of Amy Duny and Rose Cullender standing at the end of the bed. Later on she became dumb and could not speak, even in her lucid intervals when she had no fit; this lasted for some days and at last her speech returned and she asked her mother to give her food. When she was asked why she could not speak for all this time she replied that Amy Duny would not permit her to speak.

Susan Chandler was present in court when her mother Mary Chandler gave evidence. She said that after Mr Pacy's children had been bewitched Amy Duny and Rose Cullender had been brought before Sir Edmund Bacon Bt, one of the magistrates who had given the order for the two women to be searched. Mary Chandler with five other women were appointed to carry out the search. They went to Rose Cullender's house and asked her whether she would agree to be searched. She did not object and she was stripped of everything starting from the head downwards. At the lower part of the stomach they found a tumour about an inch long and Rose said that this was a strain caused by carrying water. Upon making a further search three more tumours were found smaller than the former. Mary Chandler continued that her daughter aged 18 years was then in service in Lowestoft and that on her rising early one morning to wash herself Rose Cullender appeared to her and took her by the hand. Susan was frightened and went to find her mother who was living in the same town, and told her what had happened. Her fear brought on a stomach ache and that night she had hysterics crying out against Rose Cullender, saying that Rose was coming to her bed for her. She suffered from fits in the same way as the others, vomited crooked pins, was stricken with blindness and at another time was dumb.

Expert evidence was given by Dr Browne of Norwich, later Sir Thomas Browne the author of *Religio Medici*, who gave it as his opinion that the children were clearly bewitched and that in Denmark there had been recently an outbreak of witchcraft when the victims had been affected in the same way, vomiting crooked pins and the like. It was his opinion "That the devil in such cases did work upon the bodies of men and women upon a natural foundation (that is) to stir up and excite such humours super-abounding in their bodies to a great excess, whereby he did in an extraordinary manner affect them with such distempers as their bodies were most subject to, as particularly appeared in these children; for he conceived that their swoonings were natural, and nothing else but that they call the mother, but only heightened to a great excess by the subtlety of the devil co-operating with the malice of those which we term witches, at whose instance he doeth these villanies."

As well as the evidence certain experiments were tried with the children. Different people were brought to touch them and when they were in their fits with clenched fists nobody could force them open, but when Rose Cullender touched them they would suddenly strike out and open their hands; this happened even when the children were blindfolded with their own aprons. To test this Hale asked Lord Cornwallis, Sir Edmund Bacon, Mr Serjeant Keeling and some other gentlemen to go with one of the children who was in her fit to another part of the hall and sent for Amy Duny. The child was blindfolded and was touched by some other person not Amy Duny and immediately opened her hands. "Whereupon the gentlemen returned openly protesting that they did believe the whole transaction of this business was a mere imposture."

One or two other witnesses were called to give their experiences with Rose Cullender and Amy Duny. John Soam, a yeoman of standing said that not long ago at harvest time he had three carts bringing home the harvest and as one of the carts was driven to the fields to load the harvest it damaged one of the windows of Rose Cullender's house. She came out in a great rage and threatened him. Although there were no difficulties with the other two carts the one that had done the damage overturned two or three times that day, and stuck in a gateway and could not be moved. As a result they had to cut down the gate post to allow the cart through. When they got near the unloading point the cart could not be drawn up to it but had to be unloaded at a distance and the men found great difficulty in unloading. Others who came to help them found that their noses started bleeding with the effort. They eventually had to give up and left the unloading until the next morning when it was quite easy.

Robert Sherringham gave evidence of a similar nature that about two years ago passing along the street where Rose Cullender lived his cart damaged her house and Rose came out and threatened him that his horses would suffer for it. All the four horses died within a short period, and he had trouble with his other cattle; as soon as his sows had a litter the piglets would leap and caper and then fall down and die. He was himself afflicted with lameness for some days and also plagued with enormous lice which he could only get rid of by burning both of his suits of clothes.

The additional evidence against Amy Duny was even more remote. Richard Spencer deposed that about 1st September last he had heard Amy say in his house that the devil would not let her rest unless she was revenged on the wife of Cornelius Sandeswell. Amy Sandeswell said that about seven or eight years previously, having bought some geese, she met Amy on the way home. Amy said that if Mrs Sandeswell did not fetch her geese home they would all be destroyed. This in fact happened. Later on Mrs Sandeswell had become the tenant of a house belonging to her husband and had warned her that the chimney would fall down. She did not take much notice as the chimney was new, but shortly afterwards the chimney did in fact fall down. Finally, her brother was a fisherman and she ordered a firkin of fish from him and arranged with a boatman to bring the fish ashore with certain other articles. She asked Amy to go with her to help carry the fish, but she refused. Mrs Sandeswell therefore went to the boatman alone and he told her that nothing he could do could prevent the firkin of fish from falling into the sea and he thought it had gone to the devil. Being questioned, the boatman said that none of the other articles in the boat had behaved in this way.

The prisoners then were asked whether they had anything to say for themselves, but they had nothing material to say. The judge in summing up said that he would not repeat the evidence lest he should misinterpret it either on one side or the other.

They should ask themselves two questions: Firstly whether or no those children were bewitched? Secondly whether the prisoners at the bar were guilty of it? That there were such creatures as witches he made no doubt at all; for first the scriptures had affirmed so much. Secondly the wisdom of all nations had provided laws against such persons which is an argument of their confidence of such a crime. And such hath been the judgment of this kingdom as appears by the Act of Parliament which hath provided punishments proportionable to the quality of the offence. And he desired them strictly to observe their evidence and desired the great God of heaven to direct their hearts to this weighty thing they had in hand. For to condemn the innocent and to let the guilty go were both an abomination to the Lord.

The jury retired and returned after about half an hour, bringing in a verdict of guilty on the thirteen charges upon which they had been indicted.

As soon as Amy Duny had been found guilty Dorothy Durent, William's mother, was restored to the use of her limbs and went home without using her crutches. The jury brought in their verdict on Tuesday 13th March 1664 in the afternoon, and the next morning the children with their parents went to the judge's lodgings. All of them spoke perfectly and were in good health except Susan Chandler, who was very thin and wan. Mr Pacy told the judge that less than half an hour after the conviction they were all restored to health and had a good night's rest, except Susan Chandler who continued to have stomach pains.

When the prisoners were brought back to court for sentence Anne Durent was so afraid that she would not go into court but the others went into court and confirmed what had previously been said in evidence. Judgment was then given that the prisoners should be hanged.

The report ends as follows: "They were much urged to confess but would not. That morning we departed for Cambridge, but no reprieve was granted. And they were executed on Monday the 17th of March following, but they confessed nothing."

On his arrival in Cambridge Hale wrote: "A discourse concerning the great mercy of God preserving us from the power and malice of evil angels". This discourse was published in a book entitled A collection of modern relations of matters of fact concerning witches and witchcraft upon the persons of people to which is prefixed a meditation concerning the mercy of God in preserving us from the malice and power of evil angels written by the late Lord Chief Justice Hale upon occasion of a trial of several wiches before him, London, 1693.

In the course of his argument he states that there is no doubt that there are such beings as evil spirits as both the Old and New Testaments assure us of it. This is confirmed by our own experience of the power and energy of evil spirits; evil spirits have more strength and energy as they are not encumbered by matter; this malice towards men is greater than their power, but their power is increased by their experience, subtlety, invisibility and knowledge of how to approach man. Man has power to repel evil spirits by means of his will and when the will resists evil spirits can gain no entry. Evil spirits can only inflict bodily damage by the agency of another man or a natural object. Witches are agents to inflict bodily damage on man. Unfortunately the meditation is unfinished and the argument is not taken further.

Hale's friend Richard Baxter wrote a book entitled *The certainty of the world of spirits and consequently of the immortality of souls of the malice and misery of the devils and the damned and of the blessedness of the justified.* The title page indicates that this was written as an addition to many other treatises for the conviction of Sadducees and infidels. The preface is dated 20th July 1691. The book contains a large number of examples of witchcraft but it is of particular interest in the comments on the trial of Rose Cullender and Amy Duny. Baxter remarks that the witches were condemned by Hale "which no man was more backward to do without full evidence". Baxter got the following story from Mr Emlin, a preacher in Dublin, who obtained it from a brother of Elizabeth and Deborah Pacy, then a respectable justice of the peace in Lowestoft. A worthy minister sitting by one of the girls in her fits suddenly felt a force pull one of the hooks from his breeches. Surprised and alarmed he searched for the hook and it was vomited out of her mouth by the girl.[2]

Baxter was well aware of the opportunities for false accusations, but in his view this does not affect his opinion that in truth there are evil spirits; "And I confess very many cheats of pretended possession have been discovered which have made some weak injudicious men think that all are such."[3]

Hale has been severely handled by Ewen in the eighteenth century, Campbell in the nineteenth century and in the twentieth century by such an expert as Wallace Notestein for the part he played in this trial. To form any opinion it is necessary to have some background knowledge of witchcraft in the seventeenth century. There had been laws against witchcraft or sorcery from Anglo-Saxon times,[4] but it is in the sixteenth century that legislation appears on the statute book, and in 1542 an Act was passed against witchcraft sorcery and enchantments.[5] This Act only remained in force for six years, when it was repealled in the early part of Edward VI's reign.[6] The year 1563 marks the beginning of an active period of prosecutions for witchcraft. In that year an Act was passed that those who "shall use, practise or exercise any witchcraft, enchantment, charm or sorcery whereby any person shall be killed or destroyed, their counsellors and abettors . . . shall suffer pain of death as a felon or felons".[7] Notestein says that two tendencies appear very clearly towards the end of Elizabeth's reign. On the one hand the feeling of the people against witchcraft was growing in intensity while on the other hand the Government appeared to be growing more lenient.[8] Davies thinks that the rise of the feeling against witchcraft in Elizabethan times was the result of the persecution of the Protestants under Mary.[9] Many Protestants found refuge abroad during Mary's reign at such places as Geneva, Basle, Zurich and Strasburg, where the burning of witches were frequent occurrences. Whether this is true or not, the Calvinists certainly excelled all others in their zeal against witchcraft, and the exiled English Protestants would have associated with Calvinists in Switzerland.

According to the statistics taken from the Home Circuit by Ewen the most dangerous period for witches was the decade 1598–1607, being the last six years of the reign of Elizabeth and the first four years of James I.[10] In the minds of the common people witchcraft was associated with Roman Catholicism. Reginald Scot in 1584 said: "One such sort as are said to be witches are women which be commonly old . . . poor and sullen, superstitious and Papists."[11] The Act against witchcraft of 1604 (1 James I cap. 12) was drafted by a committee of the House of Lords with the advice of Sir Edward Anderson, Chief Justice of the Common Pleas; Sir William Perryman, Chief Baron of the Exchequer; Sir Christopher Yelverton and Sir David Williams, Justices of the King's Bench; Serjeant Croke; the Attorney-General, Sir Edward Coke; and Sir John Tindall, an ecclesiastical lawyer.[12] It should be noted that this Act was passed early in the seventeenth century with the advice and approbation of judges and lawyers of the highest repute, including the greatest lawyer of his time, Sir Edward Coke. As late as 1604 witchcraft was taken very seriously by Parliament and lawyers of the day and new legislation on the subject was passed.

The Act was in wider terms than any previously passed and was directed against any person who shall

use practise or exercise any invocation or conjuration of any evil and wicked spirits or shall consult covenant with entertain employ feed or reward any evil and wicked spirit to or for any intent or purpose; or take up any dead man, woman or child out of his, her or their grave, or any other place where the dead body resteth, or the skin, bone or any part of any dead person, to be employed or used in any manner of witchcraft, sorcery, charm, or enchantment; or shall use, practise or exercise any witchcraft, enchantment, charm, or sorcery whereby any person shall be killed or destroyed, wasted, consumed, pined or lamed in his or her body or any part thereof; and every such offender or offenders, their aiders, abettors and counsellors . . . shall suffer pain of death as felon or felons, and shall lose the privilege and benefit of clergy and sanctuary.[13]

Under previous statutes it had not been possible to put a witch to death unless some death could be laid to his or her charge, but under the Act of 1604 it was only necessary to prove that the witch made use of evil spirits and some bodily injury had resulted. Of thirty-seven cases in the reign of James I where witches were sentenced to death seventeen were on indictments for witchcraft which had not caused death, and in the other twenty cases the accused were charged with murder.[14] The statute of 1604 may well have been one of the reasons for the increase of witch trials immediately following that date.

There is no doubt that James I was deeply interested in witchcraft and in 1597 published his *Daemonologie*, a defence of the belief in witchcraft resulting from two attacks on such belief by Scot and a German physician by the name of Wierus.[15] This book was influential in its time and when James I came to the throne would receive added weight as the opinion of the monarch. To prosecute witches would win the King's approval and officials and judges would be prompted to greater efforts to stamp out witchcraft.

James himself uncovered several miscarriages of justice, and after 1617 the number of witch trials fell. The worst case was that of the 'Boy of Bilston' in 1616. A boy of 12 had fits which were said to have been caused by several women whom he accused of being witches. Nine women were hanged and six more arrested. James on his way north stopped at Leicester and caused the boy to be examined. The fraud was discovered[16] and the two judges, Mr Justice Winch and Serjeant Crewe, were disgraced.[17]

The attitude of Charles I towards witchcraft resembled that of James I during the latter part of his reign. The only notable witch trial was the trial of Lancashire witches in 1633, which was an outcome of the trial of the Lancaster witches in 1612. Prosecutions for witchcraft increased during the period of the Commonwealth, rising to a peak in the year 1645, when the notorious witchfinder

Matthew Hopkins was most active. He was an attorney at Ipswich and it is probable that witchfinding was good business and a method of extending his practice. He was not content with remaining in his own county of Suffolk but extended his activities to Norfolk, Cambridgeshire, Northamptonshire, Huntingdonshire and Bedfordshire. He accused so many people of witchcraft that he stirred up opposition, but fortunately he died of consumption some time in 1647.[18]

During the period of the Commonwealth executions were numerous from 1649–53, but from 1653–9 there was a rapid falling off both in executions and accusations.[19] Pollock and Maitland considered the period of the Commonwealth "as the worst days for witches in England",[20] but this opinion was formed before the researches of Ewen were undertaken. Ewen states that so far as he can estimate from existing records there were more trials in the forty-two years of the reign of Elizabeth than during the entire seventeenth century.[21] Notestein takes the view that the Commonwealth government was not greatly interested in witchcraft but inclined towards leniency.[22] Certainly Cromwell's government tried to mitigate the severity of the criminal law. There appears to have been a steady decline in the number of executions for witchcraft from Elizabethan times with the exception of the period around 1645 when Matthew Hopkins was active.

After the Restoration witches were still being accused and brought to trial throughout the kingdom. On 3rd September 1660 Joan Neville was found guilty of murder by witchcraft by Sir Orlando Bridgeman at Kingston-upon-Thames Assizes, although it is doubtful whether she was executed.[23] The last execution in England traced by Ewen was that of Alice Molland who was tried at the Exeter Lent Assizes in 1684 before Sir Francis North, Chief Justice of the Common Pleas, and Sir Thomas Raymond, a judge of the King's Bench.[24] There is no doubt that Sir John Holt, Chief Justice of the King's Bench from 1689–1710 did more than any other judge to end the prosecution of witches, and he secured the acquittal of witches at no less than eleven trials.[25] He had a reputation for detecting false pretences of every kind and his talents were used to good effect in pointing out the various discrepancies in the evidence to the jury.

There were special rules for the examination of witches, for clearly the evidence was different from that required in the case of other suspected felons. Michael Dalton, a Master in Chancery, in his book *The County Justice*, first printed in 1618, had a section on the "Discovery of Witches"[26] and the basic principles and ideas are as follows:

1. Witches have a familiar spirit which appears to them sometimes in the form of a man or woman or an animal such as a toad.
2. The spirit has some place on the body such as a teat where it sucks.
3. Witches often have models in clay or wax of the person they are bewitching found in their house or buried by them.
4. Witches are given to cursing and threatening revenge which subsequently occurs.
5. Their implicit confession such as "I have not hurt you as yet" or "You should have let me alone."
6. Frequent enquiries about a sick person especially when forbidden to enter the house.
7. Appearance to a sick person in his fits.
8. The sick person in his fits naming the suspected witch.
9. The common report of their neighbours, especially if the suspected witch is a relative or servant of a convicted witch.
10. Evidence of other witches confessing their own witchcraft and accusing suspected witches of having spirits or marks, having been at their meetings, confessing what harm they have done.
11. If a dead body bleeds on being touched by a witch.
12. The death of the person bewitched.
13. The evidence and confessions of children or servants of witches.
14. The voluntary confession of the witch about what she has done.
15. The stench from a witch's house.
16. Sudden sickness without any apparent cause.
17. Two or more people having identical fits.
18. When a sick person in his fits foretells what the witch or other absent persons are doing or saying.
19. Where sick persons do not remember afterwards what was said in their fits.
20. When a child or weak person has supernatural strength so that strong men are unable to keep him in his bed.
21. When the party vomits up crooked pins, needles, coals, lead, straw, hair or the like.
22. When the party has some misfortune in a dream and this subsequently befalls him.

With this background the part played by Hale in the trial of 1664 can be more easily understood.

Hale would take at face value any references to witches in the Bible. Most references to witches are in the Old Testament. "Thou shall not suffer a witch to live" (Exodus, Ch. 22, v. 18). "A man also or a woman that hath a familiar spirit, or that is a wizard, shall surely be put to death; they shall stone them with stones" (Leviticus, Ch. 20, v. 27). "There shall not be found among you anyone that useth divination or an observer of times or an enchanter or a witch or a charmer or a consulter with familiar spirits or a necromancer" (Deuteronomy, Ch. 18, v. 10, 11). In his charges to the jury Hale stated that he had no doubt that there were such creatures as witches as the scriptures affirmed it. To a man such as Hale who believed in the supernatural and the revelations contained in the scriptures this would be irrefutable evidence.

All other nations had laws against witches. This would be regarded as weighty evidence by Hale as he set great store by the accumulated wisdom of mankind.

There had been an Act of Parliament on this subject only sixty years before, drawn up by the advice of eminent lawyers including Sir Edward Coke. How could a judge with Hale's education and background be expected to deny his religion, his experiences and a recent Act of Parliament?

The real gravamen of the charge against Hale is not that he believed in witches but that he did not sum up to the jury against conviction in this particular case in 1664. There was undoubtedly a *prima facie* case of witchcraft against both Amy Duny and Rose Cullender. In Amy's case there was evidence that the child Elizabeth Durent complained about Amy in her fits; Amy visited the house and was turned out by the angry mother; Amy threatened that the child would not live long and the child died. Deborah Pacy became ill after Amy had gone to the house to buy herrings and had been refused. The child cried out in her fits that Amy and Rose were the cause of her illness and vomited bent pins and nails. The father Samuel Pacy anxious to send the children away for a change of scene sent them to his sister Margaret Arnold who was clearly sceptical and took the pins out of their clothes and sewed them up instead. Anne Durent became ill after Rose Cullender had gone to her father's house to buy herrings and was refused. She said she had seen Rose in her fits and vomited pins. Mary Chandler was instructed by the magistrate to search the two women and she gave evidence of examining Rose and finding a tumour an inch long at the lower part of the stomach. Expert evidence was given by Dr Thomas Browne of Norwich, who gave as his opinion that the children were clearly bewitched. On the other hand an experiment was made at Hale's request when a child reacted to the touch of some other person in the same way as if that person had been a witch. The gentlemen who conducted the experiment clearly thought the whole accusation was a fraud and said so.

A summing up is a recapitulation of the evidence by the judge drawing the attention of the jury to the salient points. Hale said that he would not repeat the evidence lest he should misinterpret it on one side or the other. He told the jury that there were such creatures as witches and that they were to ask themselves two questions: whether or not the children were bewitched and whether the prisoners were guilty of bewitching them. The jury had heard all the evidence and it was for them to decide. It is not possible from reading the report to discover whether Hale was satisfied with the evidence or not. To say that Hale failed to sum up strongly against acquittal is to misunderstand the whole position. He would have regarded such action as usurping the functions of the jury. It was for the judge to tell the jury what the law was and for the jury to find the facts. It was the duty of the judge to refrain from making any comments which might influence the jury in coming to their decision. Hale's attitude to summing up may well be unique stemming from his strict probity and anxiety not to misrepresent any of the facts to the jury.

Hale's attitude towards witchcraft is compared very unfavourably with that of Sir John Holt. Notesein says: "without doubt Chief Justice Holt did more than any other man in English history to end the prosecution of witches".[27] One of his best known witch cases was the trial of Richard Hathaway as a cheat and impostor in 1702 (State Trials, vol. XIV, p. 639). Richard Hathaway, the apprentice to a blacksmith, Thomas Welling, was subject to fits and was accused of pretending to be bewitched by Sarah Murdoch. He claimed that only by scratching Sarah Murdoch could he be freed from his fits and fasting. A clergyman from Southwark, Dr Martin, was asked to come and pray with him but, thinking Hathaway was a fraud, arranged for him to scratch another woman and straightaway Hathaway was cured of his fit and could take food. Sarah Murdoch continued to be persecuted by the rabble and fled from Southwark and took lodgings in London. She was not allowed to rest in peace and was brought to trial as a witch and acquitted. Hathaway continued his persecution, claiming corruption both of judge and jury and Sarah remained in danger of her life from the mob. Hathaway was arrested and put in the charge of Mr Kensy, a medical man in Fetter Lane, who was instructed to examine him and make a report for the court. Although he was supposed to be fasting the maid supplied him with food, saying she had quarrelled with her master. At the trial there was evidence that he secreted pins in his clothing for use when vomiting, but when the chamber pot was held by someone else no pins appeared in it. Holt summed up very strongly against Hathaway and the jury found him guilty without retiring.

There is no doubt at all that in a case of this nature there would have been a conviction if the trial had taken place before Hale. Holt had no inhibitions about summing up trenchantly, but in the particular circumstances of Hathaway's case the evidence was so clear that a jury with Hale as judge would have convicted. It must be remembered in comparing the attitudes of Hale and Holt that Holt was operating thirty years later than Hale when public opinion was changing and that Holt presided over many more witch trials than Hale. Hale certainly conducted the trial at Bury St Edmunds and possibly the trial of Isabel Rigby in Lancaster in March 1669 when Isabel Rigby was sentenced to death by Hale for bewitching two neighbours at Hindley,[28] but we have no evidence of any others. Hutchinson records six trials presided over by Holt[29] and states that witches were acquitted by him on eleven occasions so that his experience in conducting this kind of trial was certainly greater than Hale's. Holt had a more sceptical nature than Hale and was more a man of the world. He had no scruples about leading a jury to his way of thinking and summing up strongly against a conviction if minded to do so. Nevertheless it does seem to be a sign of weakness in Hale that he failed to sum up the evidence and point out to the jury the failure of the experiment. His conduct on this occasion indicates the credulity and superstition which mingled with his religious beliefs.

NOTES

1 See also *A Tryal of Witches at the Assizes held at Bury St Edmunds by a person then attending the court.* This report is repeated verbatim in *6 State Trials.*
2 R. Baxter, *The Certainty of the Worlds of Spirits*, p. 80.
3 ibid., p. 3.
4 R. T. Davies, *Four Centuries of Witch-belief*, p. 13.
5 33 Henry VIII cap. 8 1542.
6 Wallace Notestein, *A History of Witchcraft in England from 1588–1718*, p. 12.
7 ibid., p. 14.
8 ibid., p. 52.
9 Davies, *Four Centuries of Witch-belief*, p. 15.
10 C. L'Estrange, Ewen, *Witch Hunting and Witch Trials*, p. 31.
11 Davies, *Four Centuries of Witch-belief*, p. 21, n. 2.
12 ibid., p. 22.
13 Ewen, *Witch Hunting and Witch Trials*, p. 20.
14 Notestein, *Witchcraft in England*, p. 105.
15 ibid., p. 97.
16 ibid., p. 140.
17 *Calendar of State Papers (Domestic) 1611–18*, p. 398.

18   Davies, *Four Centuries of Witch-belief*, p. 153.
19   Notestein, *Witchcraft in England*, p. 206.
20   Sir Frederick Pollock and Frederick Maitland, *The History of English Law*, 2nd ed., vol. 2, p. 556.
21   Ewen, *Witch Hunting and Witch Trials*, preface xii.
22   Notestein, *Witchcraft in England*, p. 206.
23   Ewen, *Witch Hunting and Witch Trials*, p. 43.
24   ibid., p. 43.
25   Notestein, *Witchcraft in England*, p. 320.
26   Ewen, *Witch Hunting and Witch Trials*, appendix II, p. 267.
27   Notestein, *Witchcraft in England*, p. 320.
28   Davies, *Four Centuries of Witch-belief*, p. 177.
29   Francis Hutchinson, *An Historical Essay Concerning Witchcraft*, p. 41.

VIII

The Fire and After 1666

The summer of 1666 was hot and dry and followed the dreadful days of the plague of 1665. In the early autumn of 1666 what Dryden called the 'Belgian wind' blew for days from the east. The City of London was dry and short of water.

On 2nd September 1666 Pepys wrote as follows in his diary: "2nd (Lord's Day) Some of our maids sitting up late last night to get things ready against our feast to-day, Jane called us up about three in the morning to tell us of a great fire they saw in the City. So I rose and slipped on my night-gown, and went to her window; and thought it to be on the Bank side of Mark Lane at the farthest; but being unused to such fires as followed I thought it far enough off; and so went to bed again and to sleep."

At that time the bakery and houses belonging to Farynor, the King's baker in Pudding Lane, was ablaze. Farynor looked at his oven at 10 p.m. on 1st September before going to bed and the embers seemed to him to be dead. Two hours later on, he, his son and his daughter, arose choking with smoke and very shortly after the Star Inn in Fish Street Hill with its wooden galleries round the yard caught fire. At 3 a.m. Sir Thomas Bludworth the Lord Mayor was fetched from his house on the other side of the City but failed to appreciate the gravity of the situation and returned home to bed.

The most inflammable area in the City was the area stretching westwards along Thames side from London Bridge as it contained many timber warehouses, sheds and small factories. Fishmongers' Hall by London Bridge was well ablaze by mid-morning. Pepys describes the confusion: "Everybody endeavouring to remove their goods and flinging into the river, or bringing them into lighters that lay off; poor people staying in their houses as long or till the very fire touched them, and then running into boats, or clambering from one pair of stairs, by the waterside, to another. And among other things, the poor pigeons, I perceive, were loth

to leave their houses but hovering above the windows and bal-
conies till they burned their wings, and fell down."

The Lord Mayor was on the scene again soon after dawn but refused to give any orders to pull down houses to prevent the spread
of the fire. All he would say was "who shall pay the charge of rebuilding the houses?" By an old law whoever pulled down a house
in the city had to bear the cost of its rebuilding, and consequently
the Lord Mayor required the owner's consent. Pepys reported to
Charles II, who ordered the Lord Mayor to pull down houses
wherever necessary. The Duke of York and Lord Arlington promised
to send troops. Pepys on his return to the city found the sorry
tide of refugees fleeing from the City laden with household goods
and valuables while the sick were carried on their beds.

By midday on Sunday nearly half Upper Thames Street was
ablaze. The King and his brother, the Duke of York, arrived by
royal barge at Queenshythe where they landed and ordered houses
to be pulled down but at nightfall the fire continued to rage un-
abated. The fire continued throughout Monday 3rd September,
when the Royal Exchange and Cornhill were destroyed and the
fire got completely out of control. The Duke of York was given
overall charge, assisted by the Earl of Craven and others, and a
headquarters was set up in Ely Place. The great cloud of yellowish
grey smoke rolled westward over the suburbs as far as Oxford,
shutting out the sun and daylight for many miles to the west.

By Wednesday the 5th September the fire had travelled from
Tower Wharf in the east to Temple Bar and had destroyed
practically everything in its path. Now it was beginning to die
down as the east wind had dropped and the efforts of the fire-
fighters were beginning to take effect. By Friday or Saturday the
great fire had burnt itself out or been extinguished.

About 100,000 people out of a population of 600,000 were
made homeless and had lost their livelihood and everything they
possessed. There was no fire insurance and no redress, and for
thousands it meant complete ruin. The homeless were encamped
on Moorfields, Tower Hill and other open spaces around the city
with their pathetic bundles of belongings. The King issued two
proclamations ordering magistrates and Deputy Lieutenants of
food-producing counties to send supplies to London, and churches,
chapels and public buildings were used for the storage of goods.

It is unlikely that Hale would be in London during the Fire as it
was during the Long Vacation, but he would be back in London in
the Michaelmas Term in November 1666.

The greatest aid to the rebuilding of London was given by an
Act of Parliament 18 and 19 Charles II cap. 7 which set up the

Court of Fire Judges and received the Royal Assent on 8th February 1667. The object was to deal with disputes in a summary manner and speed up the rebuilding. The Act is believed to have been drafted by Hale and is short and to the point. Under the ordinary law of the land many tenants would have been liable to action in the courts to compel them to rebuild and reinstate their buildings under the terms of their leases. This would clearly be inequitable when a tenant had lost everything in the fire and there was no fire insurance to help him. The principle behind the Act was that landlord and tenant should each bear a fair proportion of the cost of reinstatement.

By the Act three or more of His Majesty's judges were authorized to hear and determine all differences between landlords, tenants, occupiers and others concerned relating to buildings lost in the fire. All the judges of the three Common Law Courts, namely the Court of King's Bench, the Court of Common Pleas, and the Court of the Exchequer, numbering twelve, were *ex officio* members of the court. There was no appeal except by leave of the two Chief Justices and Chief Baron and then to a full court of seven judges. The court was constituted a court of record and the statute provided that the judgments should be entered in books of parchment and signed by three or more of the judges which books were to be kept in the custody of the Mayor and Aldermen of the City of London. The registrar of the court was one Stephen Mandy, who wrote out the decrees on paper and examined them before they were engrossed on parchment.

The court sat in the hall at Clifford's Inn and it was fitted up as a court at the modest cost of £21 0s. 3d.[1] The following articles were delivered at Clifford's Inn for the use of the judges on 1st January 1667:

	£	s.	d.
22 skines of parchment ruled according to order	1	16	8
3 Remes of ye finest Amsterdam Armes	1	19	0
300 of seckond quilles		4	0
1 bage of sand		1	0
1 botell of inke of 3 quarts and botell		5	0
1 brasele (brazilwood) ruler		1	1
Pd ye carpenter to alter ye benche and mend sundries	1	2	0
Pd ye talowchandler for canles (candles)	1	8	0
Pd ye Char Coleman for 24 sacks of Charcole at 2s. 4d.	2	16	0

Sittings began on 27th February 1667, and during the first year the court sat on 120 days with a vacation from the 19th July to 7th October the judges making over 400 attendances and disposing of 374 cases.[2] The court sat on three or four days each week and very often on Saturday. Hale heard 140 cases and in most of them the hearing did not take more than one day. Adjournments were given to enable an absent defendant to appear, to give time for an agreed settlement, for the production of documents or attendance of witnesses. The court disliked adjournments and often proceeded in the absence of parties "so that the refractoriness of the defendants should not obstruct rebuilding". Service of the summons was made by a court official. The court was greatly helped by counsel and there appears to have been some members of the bar who specialized in this work, Mr Sturges appearing in 125 cases, Mr Jenner in 61, and Mr Bowes in 56. Very often counsel would embody the terms of settlement in a formal agreement for approval by the court. Nevertheless it was not essential to employ counsel and many parties appeared in person.

The court had power to cancel existing agreements and substitute a fresh agreement, to order new leases or to extend the terms of existing leases by not more than forty years. The Act protected tenants from landlords who required their rent although the tenant's premises had been destroyed and he had no means to pay. The cases were to be heard speedily without the payment of fees, the judges receiving no payment for their work. The principle behind the Act was that everyone concerned should bear a proportionate part of the loss, and such were the individual differences of circumstances that it was impossible to lay down any general rule of law. The court first tried to find out whether the landlord or tenant was best able to rebuild speedily and the agreement was drafted accordingly. If the landlord had the money to rebuild he was to receive a fair and economic rent from the tenant, while if the tenant rebuilt this was borne in mind when fixing the rent and the length of the term. When a tenant had lost everything and did not want a new lease the court would cancel his lease or order the payment of a small sum to the landlord to extinguish the lease.

The main purpose of the Act was to facilitate rebuilding quickly but the court did in practice give preference to the person in occupation at the time of the fire if he had the means to rebuild.[3] For example, although the Dean and Chapter of St Paul's wished to build houses for the residentiaries of the cathedral on their land in St Bennet's Hill, the court declared in favour of their lessee who wished to rebuild. The court ruled that a tenant in possession or a shopkeeper who wished to return to his shop should be able to do so and that it was for the public good that old inhabitants should be able to go back to their former homes and trade. The court frequently required the house to be rebuilt by a certain fixed date such as Michaelmas 1668 and sometimes "with all convenient speed". The date for the first payment of rent was usually specified in the order being one year from the date of the order and this was consequently an incentive for speedy building. In some cases boundaries were amended and sites enlarged and alternative sites provided for joint development. Restrictions and change of user were considered, and in one case the court decided that a victualling house was not proper in Lombard Street and in another that an inn should be rebuilt in Friday Street as this would be good for business.[4]

The decisions of the court not only decided the particular case but provided precedents to enable parties to come to terms without coming to the court. When both landlord and tenant were ruined by the catastrophe there was a provision in the Act that any sites not built on after the lapse of three years should after nine months' notice be taken by the City Corporation and sold, the proceeds being handed over to those entitled.

The first case on 27th February 1667 was heard by Hale, Baron Atkins, Baron Turnor and Justice Archer. William Coates a wine merchant was an assignee of a lease of a warehouse and cellar in Seething Lane for five years from Midsummer 1665 at £25 per annum. Coates wanted to rebuild provided that his lease was extended but Nathaniel Withers the landlord refused to agree as the premises were intermixed with other premises of his which he wished to rebuild. The court ordered Coates to pay Withers £25 for the surrender of his lease and deliver up possession on 28th March 1667. Coates was relieved from the payment of rent since 24th June 1666 and discharged from his covenants under the lease.

Hale sat again on 20th, 21st, 27th and 28th March, possibly during the Easter vacation. On the 28th March the case of Thomas Rivers *v.* Rector and Churchwardens of St Nicholas Cole Abbey was heard. Rivers had bought a lease of thirty-one years from 24th June 1666 for £160 at a rent of £20 per annum and had spent £200 on improvements. Agreed terms were approved by the court for a new lease for seventy years from Midsummer 1668 at a rent of £15 per annum, Rivers doing the rebuilding.

In gratitude to the judges for hearing the cases without fee and to the general satisfaction, the Common Council ordered full length portraits of the judges to be painted by Michael Wright at a cost of £60 each. It was the speedy determination of the litigation which enabled the city to be rebuilt without undue delay. The success of the Act was largely due to Hale. Apart from drafting the Bill he was responsible for settling the procedure and took a full share in the work of the court.

NOTES

1   Philip E. Jones (ed.), *Fire Court*, vol. I, p. ix.
2   ibid., p. xi.
3   ibid., p. xv.
4   ibid., p. xviii.

IX

Richard Baxter 1667

It was not until 1667 that Hale and Richard Baxter met, but very soon a warm friendship grew up between the two men. Baxter left some notes on the life of Hale which were published as an appendix to Burnet's life. Baxter was a Presbyterian clergyman of the Church of England who conformed for as long as his conscience permitted him to do so. He was an upright man, a learned and able preacher, persuasive with his tongue and pen, although inclined to be verbose. He suffered a good deal of physical pain without complaint, but his disposition seems to have been somewhat cold.

After the Fire of London Hale was looking for a house outside the City and at that time a small group of Puritans were living at Acton in Middlesex. Acton was called the place of the oaks on account of the great forest of oaks which lay about it, and Middlesex was a county "very pleasant and healthy to which fine gravelly soil does not a little contribute".[1] It was to this pleasant place that Hale came in 1667 where he expected to be amongst congenial neighbours. There may well have been a shortage of accommodation in London, but the reason why he set up house in Acton at this time was the occasion of his second marriage. He had been a widower for nine years and he married as his second wife Anne Bishop, daughter of Joseph Bishop. Burnet says that she came from Fawley in Berks, but there is no record of her birth in the Fawley parish registers. She appears to have taken her father to live with her at Acton, as the Acton parish registers record that on 13th October 1670 Mr Bishop was buried from Lord Chief Baron Hale's house.

Hale attended the Parish Church of St Mary regularly every Sunday, but Baxter did not at first seek his acquaintance. A friend of Baxter's, Serjeant Fountain, asked him why he did not visit Hale and Baxter replied that he had no occasion to pay a visit and he thought Hale might be embarrassed meeting someone who was unpopular with the clergy. The Serjeant replied that it was not etiquette for Hale to visit him and that he Baxter should make the first move, which he did.

Baxter lived in a small house which had formerly been in the occupation of Major-General Skippon, Cromwell's Major-General for the London District in 1655. It had "a pleasant backside", which meant "a fruitful field, grove and garden, surrounded by a remarkably high deeply founded and long extended wall". Hale was very attracted by the house and garden and wanted to buy it. Baxter's landlord wanted to sell, but Hale would not approach him until he made enquiries through a third party to find out whether Baxter wanted to leave. Baxter said he was prepared to go as the landlord had to sell, and Baxter took a larger house near the parish church. No trace of Hale's house remains nor of the parish church, which was rebuilt in the Victorian fashion in 1865. The only visible connection with Acton lies in a small stone head of Hale at the side of the front porch, put there by the builders of the present church, and the parish rate book, which shows that Hale paid 4s. 3d. rates in 1674 and 9s. 11d. in 1675.

Hale and Baxter frequently met after this and, according to Baxter, their discussions were usually on philosophical subjects. Hale was apparently a keen collector of books both new and old, especially those on philosophy. Neither of them approved of everything that Aristotle said, but Hale thought more of Aristotle than Baxter did. Hale said that it had become the fashion for men at the universities to decry Aristotle but he doubted whether any of these men had really studied him. It required a great deal of study to know what he taught and it was far easier just to skim through what the critics had written about him. Hale constantly returns to this theme, that where science is concerned (in which he would include law) it is necessary to have a full knowledge of the subject before you are in a position to make useful comments and suggestions and that more is required than a good intellect and the use of reasoning.

Baxter gives a number of sidelights on Hale's personal life and habits. Hale had a passion for study and quietness and Baxter says that he shunned the visits of important people except those who had necessary business with him and grudged every interruption on his privacy. He says that Hale's speech was slow and slightly hesitating at times. Hale usually chose the subject for discussion and would put forward all the difficulties and objections but not give his own opinion. He never interrupted Baxter in the course of his argument and was prepared to change his mind and be convinced by the force of the argument.

Naturally the conversation frequently turned to religion; Baxter says that although they were friends he had no idea what time Hale spent on his personal devotions and Hale clearly regarded this as something which must be done in secret. Hale was a member of the Church of England and attended his parish church regularly every Sunday throughout his life.

Baxter says that Hale's behaviour in church was to conform with the current practice, but he had the disconcerting habit of standing up whenever the Bible was read to make clear that the reading of the Gospels and the Epistles were all one to him and that if he stood for the Gospel he would also stand for the Epistle. His main desire was that men should not "be peevishly quarrelsome against any lawful circumstances, forms or orders in religion". Consequently, although he was sympathetic towards Non-conformists and did what he could to mitigate the severity of the laws against them, he thought that "those of the separation were good men, but they had narrow souls, who would break the peace of the Church about such inconsiderable matters as the points in difference were".

On the subject of bishops, Baxter and Hale agreed to differ as Hale thought that the wealth and power of the bishops enabled them to come to the relief of the poor, to protect the clergy and "to keep up the honour of religion in the world". Baxter was much more sceptical about the value of wealth and position and pointed out that the best men were not tempted by wealth and honour but it was a great temptation for men of inferior qualities. It was these men who usually secured the bishoprics and they were not free with their wealth to the poor nor did they assist the clergy to any great extent. About the inferior clergy Baxter said: "I can truly say that he [Hale] greatly lamented the negligence, and ill lives, and violence of some of the clergy; and would oft say 'What have they their calling honour and maintenance for, but to seek the instructing and saving of men's souls.' "

Hale observed the Sabbath strictly and there was an element of superstition in this strictness. He told Baxter that when he was young he was in the West Country and heard that a relative in London was sick and he had to go to London to attend to urgent business affairs. He set off on a Sunday but fate was against him. One horse fell lame, whilst another died, which he took as a rebuke from God for travelling on a Sunday. Sabbath observance was one of the more unpleasant features of Puritan belief and the treatment of children was harsh in the extreme. One letter written to his grandchildren on 20th October 1662[2] sets out the terrors and gruelling nature of the Sabbath Day. Children must get up at least three hours before morning sermon, read two chapters of the Bible and go to private prayers. At Morning Prayer boys should be uncovered, but if the weather is cold they might wear a satin cap. It is suggested that the sermon should be written down to prevent the mind from wandering. After service they should have a moderate meal and then walk in the garden for half an hour to digest. This should be followed by a period in their own room studying sermon notes and meditating until the next church service. If they were well there was Evening Prayer to attend and there should be no laughing, whispering or gazing about. They should return immediately to their room after service for further meditation and Bible reading and if the sermon is not repeated in their father's house go to the minister's house to hear it repeated there. After supper and family prayers they should say their own prayers in private before going to bed. Needless to say there was no time for bowling, shooting, hunting, merry talk, feastings and fancy food, all of which were forbidden. Works of absolute necessity might be done such as stopping a break in a sea-wall, shoring up a house in danger of falling, pulling an ox out of a ditch, setting a broken bone, feeding cattle and preparing food; while works of charity may be carried out, such as relieving the poor, giving medicine, visiting the afflicted, admonishing the disorderly, making peace between neighbours and settling minor differences.

After Baxter moved to his new house near the church he was in the habit of preaching in his own house after Morning Prayer in the parish church. The rector of the parish was Dr Reeves, Dean of Windsor, Dean of Wolverhampton, Parson of Horsley and Chaplain-in-Ordinary to the King. Naturally he was seldom present at services at Acton, which were conducted by the curate, described by Baxter as "a weak, dull young man, that spent most of his time in ale houses, and read a few dry sentences to the people but once a day". Dr Reeves was pleased that Baxter came to church bringing others with him, but he was not at all pleased when he saw people crowding into Baxter's house after matins.

By the Conventicle Act of 1663 it was an offence to go to any separate meeting for religious worship where more than five persons were present besides the family. The Act expired at the end of October, 1668 and prior to that date Baxter had been careful to keep strictly within the law.[3] After the Act expired he opened his house to all who wished to come, and crowds attended from Brentford and the neighbouring parishes. Hale thought the preaching was helpful and publicly showed his approval. Colonel

G

Phillips, a neighbour, complained but nothing was done at first. Matters came to a head when a former rector, the Reverend John Reynolds, in conversation with the local apothecary, Mr Brace-girdle, was provoked into saying that the Non-conformists were not so contemptible in number and quality as Bracegirdle made out and he was surprised that Bracegirdle, living in Acton, was so hot against them as meetings were held in a private house next door to the church. Bracegirdle informed Dr Reeves, who told the King. The King had Mr Reynolds questioned and instructed Dr Reeves to apply to the Bishop of London to have the meeting suppressed. The Bishop laid the information before two Brent-ford magistrates, Thomas Ross and J. Phillips, who issued a warrant for Baxter's arrest on 9th June 1669. Baxter told Hale about the warrant but did not ask his advice, nor was any opinion given.[4] Although the Act of 1663 had expired, a case against Baxter could be made under the Elizabethan Statute 35 Elizabeth I.

On 11th June Baxter appeared before the justices at Brentford. The public was excluded and also the clerk to the magistrates.[5] They told Baxter that he was guilty of keeping a conventicle con-trary to the law and asked him to take the Oxford oath: "I A.B. do swear that it is not lawful upon any any pretence whatsoever to take arms against the king; and that I do abhor that traitorous position of taking arms by his authority against his person, or against those that are commissioned by him in pursuance of such commissions; and that I will not at any time endeavour any altera-tion of government either in Church or State." This oath included the words, "I will not at any time endeavour any alteration of government in the Church", and Baxter refused to subscribe to this He pressed for witnesses to be called to substantiate the charge and, as he presumed it was a court of justice, that the public should be admitted. Both these requests were refused and Baxter was found guilty of preaching in an unlawful assembly and committed to the New Prison at Clerkenwell for six months. He refused to give an undertaking not to preach on the Sunday and was therefore taken to prison on the next day Saturday, 12th June. He wrote in his life: "And so I finally left that place, being grieved that Satan had prevailed to stop the poor people in such hopeful beginnings of a common reformation, and that I was to be deprived of the exceeding grateful neighbourhood of the Lord Chief Baron Hale who could scarce refrain from tears when he did hear of the first warrant for my appearance."[6] Before he went to prison Hale gave Baxter four books in folio which he had written on religious subjects. Baxter comments: "The only fault I found with them of any moment was that great copiousness, the effect of his fullness and patience, which will be called tediousness by impatient readers."

On his way to prison Baxter called to see his friend Serjeant Fountain, who read the warrant and advised him to apply for the issue of a writ of habeas corpus. He suggested that he should not apply to the Court of King's Bench, as the judges would be against him, nor to the Court of the Exchequer, as this might be an embarrassment to his friend Hale, but to the Court of Common Pleas. Baxter was well treated in prison. He had a large room and permission to walk in the garden, but there were drawbacks. The room he had was over the gate and he could get very little sleep on account of the comings and goings of prisoners during the night. During the day he had so many visitors that he had no time for study or reflection.

The judges of the Court of Common Pleas at that time were Chief Justice Vaughan, Judge Tyrell, Judge Archer and Judge Wild. Hale spoke openly in favour of Baxter at dinner at Serjeant's Inn, not on the question of law but as to his character.[7] All the judges found technical defects in the warrant and Chief Justice Vaughan said that the names of the witnesses should be inserted. Baxter had carefully prepared his case on the particular circumstances, but this was not considered by the court. All the justices had to do was to start all over again and avoid technical errors. Baxter had the rent of his house in Acton to pay, but could not live there and decided to leave Middlesex so that he could be more than five miles from Acton and the City of London. The justices instructed counsel to prepare a new warrant naming 4th June as the day when Baxter had preached but not naming any witnesses. The warrant was served and Baxter was not taken to Clerkenwell but to the common jail at Newgate, which, apart from the dungeon at the Tower, had the reputation for being the worst prison in the land. No further application for a writ of habeas corpus having been made, he appears to have served his sentence and on his release found a house at Totteridge near Barnet. In the next session of Parliament a bill against conventicles was brought in which applied to Baxter, and he was compelled to leave the country and live abroad. After he had gone abroad he corresponded with Hale on philosophical and religious subjects, and Hale remembered him in his will giving him a legacy of 40s., with which Baxter "purchased the largest Cambridge Bible and put his picture before it as a monument to my house".[8]

NOTES

1 Frederick J. Powicke, *The Rev. Richard Baxter under the Cross* (*1662–1691*).
2 Letters to his grandchildren, ch. 9, B. M. Harl MS. 4009.
3 Frederick J. Powicke, *The Rev. Richard Baxter under the Cross* (*1662–1691*), p. 37.
4 ibid., p. 35 .
5 Richard Baxter, *Reliquiae Baxterianae*, p. 48 .
6 ibid., p. 50.
7 ibid., p. 59.
8 ibid., p. 181.

X

The Comprehension 1668

With the fall of the Earl of Clarendon in 1667 the outlook became brighter for the Non-conformists. The penal laws were relaxed, and when the King spoke in Parliament on 10th February 1668 he said, "One thing more I hold myself obliged to recommend to you at this present, that is that you would anxiously think of some course to beget a better union and composure in the minds of my Protestant subjects in matters of religion whereby they may be inclined to submit quietly to the Government, but also cheerfully give their assistance to the support of it."[1]

Non-conformists in London went openly to their meetings but, much to the King's annoyance, Parliament insisted on the penal laws being enforced. Clarendon was succeeded by Sir Orlando Bridgeman as Lord Keeper and the latter, knowing his royal master's wishes, made one further attempt at Church unity. He had always been a Royalist but was a first-class lawyer and had been permitted by Cromwell to practise as a conveyancer.

He convened a small committee to consider some scheme of unity, and Baxter, who was a member of the committee, said that the Presbyterians consisted of himself, Thomas Manton and William Bates, whilst the Church of England members were Hezekiah Burton and John Wilkins.

The two other Presbyterians apart from Baxter had the same background. Both had worked for the return of the King and both had refused preferment in the Church from the King. William Bates was an eloquent preacher, Thomas Manton a popular leader of the Presbyterians, and both were moderates.

On the Church of England side Hezekiah Burton was a Fellow of Magdalene College Cambridge, as was Bridgeman, and it is likely that Bridgeman approached Burton asking him to suggest the names of suitable people to serve on the committee. Burton was certainly a friend of Bridgeman's because when Bridgeman became Lord Keeper in 1667 he appointed Burton to a stall in Norwich Cathedral.

The most distinguished member of the committee was John Wilkins. He had the keenest interest in mathematics, mechanics, astronomy and natural sciences, and was a member of a group of like-minded men who met in London in 1645 to carry out scientific experiments. When he was appointed Warden of Wadham College Oxford by Cromwell in 1648 his lodgings were the scene of further meetings and experiments.[2] These men later became the founder members of the Royal Society. At Wadham Wilkins gained the confidence of both the Government and the Royalists by his moderation, and many Royalists sent their sons to be educated at his college. After the Restoration Wilkins returned to London, where he was noticed by the King who took a great personal interest in scientific research and in 1662 he was appointed Bishop of Chester.

The Committee met on a number of occasions and certain proposals were made by the Church of England members which were eventually agreed by the Presbyterians:

1. That such ministers who had been ordained only by the Presbyterians should have the imposition of hands by the Bishop with this form of words: "Take thou authority to preach the word of God, and administer the Sacraments in any congregation of the Church of England where thou shalt be lawfully appointed thereunto."
2. In substitution for all former oaths of allegiance ministers should subscribe: "I A.B. do hereby profess and declare that I approve the doctrines, worship, and government established in the Church of England as containing all things necessary to salvation; and that I will not endeavour by myself, or any others, directly or indirectly, to bring in any doctrine contrary to that which is established. And I do hereby promise, that I will continue in the Communion of the Church of England, and will not do anything to disturb the peace thereof."
3. That the gesture of kneeling at the Sacrament, the cross in baptism and bowing at the name of Jesus be optional or abolished altogether.
4. That if the liturgy and canons be altered in favour of dissenters then every preacher, upon his institution shall declare his assent to the lawfulness of the use of it, and promise that it shall be constantly used at the usual time and place.

Having reached agreement the problem was to put the agreement into legal form and Baxter, by reason of his friendship with Hale and knowing of his keen interest, suggested that Hale should be asked to prepare a Bill for Parliament. Hale drafted the Bill for presentation to Parliament early in 1668.

Wilkins was friendly with Seth Ward, Bishop of Salisbury, and foolishly discussed the matter with him. Wilkins and Ward, although both interested in science, did not see eye to eye on matters of Church unity. Ward was a staunch supporter of the penal laws and an enemy of the dissenters. Ward passed the word on to his brother bishops, who became alarmed and prepared counter measures. As soon as Parliament met notice was taken that there were rumours outside of an Act of Comprehension and Indulgence. It was moved and resolved that no man shall bring such an Act into the House, and consequently the Bill was killed stone dead and not even considered by the House.

There was in fact very little chance of the proposals succeeding. The bishops and clergy of the Church of England were entrenched in their freeholds and they had no desire nor was there any need for them to make any concessions to the Presbyterians. It was all very well for the King to be generous with that which was not his own but more Presbyterians in the Church of England meant more competition for preferment and livings. The Church of England party adopted a policy of non co-operation, put forward no counter proposals to those agreed with the Presbyterians and as soon as they saw that a Bill was to be considered by Parliament took steps to make sure that it was not even discussed.

It is not difficult to understand the opposition to this scheme. Royalist bishops and clergy had spent long years in exile or dispossessed from their livings which had now been restored to them. The Presbyterians of the moderate sort may have helped the return of the King but the Church of England party could not see why the King should repay them at the expense of the clergy of the Church of England. We do not know whether Hale really anticipated any success from the efforts of this committee. He was undoubtedly sympathetic to the plight of the Presbyterians and would naturally be willing to do what he could to help.

It was as a result of this committee that Hale first met Wilkins and a particularly warm friendship seems to have sprung up between the two men. They had many interests in common and Hale appears to have dined frequently with Wilkins until Wilkins' death in 1672.

From the professional point of view the most interesting case of 1668 was the trial of Peter Messenger when Hale dissented from the opinion of his brother judges. On 1st April 1668 the trial took place of Peter Messenger and others[3] on a charge of high treason in tumultuously assembling themselves in Moorfields and other places under colour of pulling down bawdy houses. The case was considered by all the judges who decided that high treason had been committed, Hale only dissenting.

The trouble started in the Easter holidays in 1668 when a number of apprentices met in East Smithfield and the idea circulated of pulling down the bawdy houses in Moorfields. It was alleged that their leader was Richard Beasley who marched at the head of a crowd of 400 or 500 with his sword drawn ably assisted by Peter Messenger carrying a green apron attached to a pole. The disturbances took place on Easter Monday, 23rd March and continued on the Tuesday and Wednesday. Surprisingly little damage seems to have been done, in view of the number of people involved and the length of time. The constable was knocked down and his staff taken away but fortunately troops arrived at the critical moment. The house of Peter Burlingham was destroyed so that a horse could have walked through it. Mrs Burlingham said that her house was not a bawdy house but that she had been dragged out and all her goods destroyed and £10 in gold taken out of her pocket.

During the course of the disturbances a party whose leader had a pike in his hand broke into the New Prison at Clerkenwell. The gaoler gave evidence that coming home he found the prison doors open. The crowd had released some of their own numbers imprisoned there and the doors were relocked by the gaoler, who refused to reopen them. The ringleader said, "We have been servants, but we will be masters now; and if you will not open the door we will do your business for you by and by."

Apart from the damage done the mob shouted slogans such as, "Down with the Redcoats", and, "If the King will not give us liberty of conscience May Day will be a bloody day." It is clear that the downfall of Clarendon had stimulated hope in the minds of the common people that there would be a relaxation of religious persecution.

Hale dissented from his brother judges on the ground that it was only an unruly company of apprentices and should not be blown up into armed rebellion against the King.[4] By a statute of Queen Mary, if any twelve or more people assembled to pull down buildings with force and remain assembled for more than two hours after a proclamation to disperse has been made it should be a felony. He argued that if pulling down buildings by a crowd had been treason at common law it would not have been necessary to have a statute to make it a felony. The law was clear that rebellion of subjects against the King was high treason, but Hale could not follow the other judges that this incident constituted such a rebellion.

About four o'clock in the afternoon of Tuesday, 9th March 1669 Hale arrived at Aylesbury for the Assizes accompanied by Serjeant Hugh Windham and on the next day, Wednesday, 10th March, the trial began of Robert Hawkins, Clerk in Holy Orders, and lately minister of Chilton.[5]

The first witness was one Larrimore, who said that on Friday, 18th September 1668 he locked the doors of his house as nobody else was at home and went out between noon and 1 p.m. to pluck hemp about a quarter of a mile away and he remained there with the rest of his family until an hour and a half after sunset. On his return home he found the doors of his house open and going to his room he could see through a chink in the loft boards Hawkins rifling a box in which there was a holland apron and a purse containing two gold rings, two pieces of gold and nineteen silver shillings. He swore that he saw Hawkins turn out the purse and take it away with all the contents except a few shillings. This evidence is corroborated by Larrimore's son and his sister Beamsley, who said that they saw Hawkins run out of Larrimore's house with a great bunch of keys and hide himself in a patch of beans and weeds. His son, the constable and another man also swore that they found a gold ring and a five-shilling piece of silver in a basket with eggs in it hanging on a pin in Hawkins' house. Finally the prosecution brought in two more witnesses, the son of Sir John Croke and Mr Good, to say that the one pawned the ring and the other the five-shilling piece to Larrimore.

The defence was based firstly on the improbability of the charge and secondly on the impossibility of its being true. Hawkins argued that if Larrimore had really been robbed he would surely have told all his neighbours. There were great discrepancies in the evidence as to the time that the robbery had taken place and Larrimore is shown to have gone for a warrant to the magistrate on the 17th September, a day before he claimed the robbery was committed. Hawkins called Samuel Brown who said that on Wednesday, 16th September, as he lay in bed early in the morning at Sir John Croke's house in Chilton, he heard a great noise and got up in alarm, as Sir John Croke was a prisoner in the Court of King's Bench and Brown was his keeper. Brown feared that an escape had been made and immediately ran downstairs and hid behind the hangings at the dining-room door. He heard Larrimore complaining to Sir John Croke that Hawkins had commenced a number of suits against him which would ruin him. Larrimore was a vehement Anabaptist and Hawkins had sued him for tithes and also for not attending church. Sir John Croke then suggested to Larrimore that he should have some gold put in Hawkins' house and then get a warrant to search the house. Having found the gold he could be charged with felony and brought before him (Sir John Croke) as a magistrate and he would send him to jail without bail and hang him at the next Assizes. After some more evidence of this nature it is reported that "Sir John Croke stole away from the bench, without taking his leave of my Lord Chief Baron, or any of the Justices".

Mr Charles Wilcox gave evidence that he was with Larrimore on Friday, 18th September from noon until nightfall at Larrimore's house in Chilton doing business about some tiles and other matters and that Hawkins was never near the house during that time. Wilcox was very carefully questioned by Hale to check the truth of his evidence.

Hale summing up to the jury said that if they believed Brown and Wilcox Larrimore's case fell to the ground. He evidently thought it a very plain case because he told the jury that there was no need for them to go from the bar, but this was a matter for them. The jury did not retire and the foreman of the jury said they were all agreed on a verdict of not guilty.

The report (written by Hawkins himself) ends: "So as soon as my trial was over, Sir John Croke, Larrimore, and the rest of that crew fled privately out of Aylesbury, and durst not stay."

It would be interesting to know why this trial was reported at all in the State Trials series, as it was only a parochial squabble of no general interest. It is of value, however, to have a detailed report of the sort of case which would commonly be dealt with at Assizes. The report is written by Hawkins himself, who was not a lawyer and probably had no knowledge of shorthand. There does appear to have been a good deal more cross-examination by the judge than would be considered proper in modern times. However in this case there was no counsel on either side and this must have been common particularly on Assize. The judge was compelled to intervene in the trial to arrive at the truth.

Hale's language according to the report is very strong when speaking about the prosecutor Larrimore. The reporter was an interested party, Hawkins, but even so the question arises whether Hale in fact used this language or not. The following remarks are reported: "Larrimore thou art a very villain"; "Come, come, Larrimore thou art a very villain; nay I think thou art the devil." After the jury had given their verdict he is reported as saying, "You have found like honest men; I do believe that he is not guilty." And he said to Larrimore, "Thou art a very villain."[6] On the first two occasions he is said to have called Larrimore a villain and a devil before the jury had come to their verdict.

The trial is of interest from two other points of view. At one stage in the trial Hale stated in open court that the same morning he had received two sugar-loaves from Sir John Croke as a present but that he had instructed the Clerk of the Assize to return them to Sir John.

The other point is of more general interest. Samuel Brown in giving evidence of the conversation between Sir John Croke and Larrimore reported Larrimore as saying, "Hawkins will undo me, for he hath entered me into most courts of England and summoned me into the Crown Office and Chancery, and I cannot maintain so many suits." Hawkins in evidence admitted that an action for tithes had been started by him against Larrimore in 1667 and a petition made in Hawkins' favour states that Hawkins had indicted Larrimore for not coming to church. Larrimore's false prosecution of Hawkins cannot be excused but it can be explained as the result of the overzealous enforcement of the penal laws by an individual incumbent.

NOTES

1   Daniel Neal, *The History of the Puritans*, vol. IV, p. 337.
2   Margery Purver, *The Royal Society: Concept and Creation*, p. 115.
3   6 *State Trials*, p. 879.
4   ibid., p. 899.
5   ibid., p. 921.
6   ibid., p. 952.

XI

Chief Justice
of the King's Bench 1671-5

On the death of Chief Justice Keyling, Hale was appointed Chief Justice of the Court of King's Bench on 18th May 1671.[1] Plaintiffs still wished for a hearing before Hale, and many cases which might have been heard by the Courts of Exchequer and Common Pleas were started in the King's Bench.

It was the custom for the marshal of the Court of King's Bench to present the judges with a piece of plate as a New Year's gift, and the Chief Justice received a larger piece than the other judges. True to form, Hale wished to refuse any gift at all, and was only prevailed on to accept the gift as this was the practice and he might prejudice the rights of future holders of the office if he refused. He insisted, however, that he should receive money instead of plate, which he sent to the prison for the relief and discharge of poor prisoners.

On July 18th 1671 the trial took place before Hale of Nathaniel John Letten and Leonar Moresco, widow, concerning the custom of merchants when an accepted bill of exchange is lost.[2] Was the accepter bound to pay the money on presentation of a second bill? It was held that the custom was that, if the first bill which is accepted is lost after acceptance but before payment, the merchant who accepted such a bill is bound to pay upon a second bill, provided that the party receiving the money gives security.

There is no proper report of this case, but the judgment has been printed. On 18th August 1671 it was sent to a City merchant, for his views, and endorsed as follows: "Sent to a merchant. You are advised seriously to peruse and examine the matters contained in this paper, and to return your thoughts thereupon in writing, wherein you agree, and wherein you differ with the reasons thereof. Pray let your answer be left at the

Benjamin Billingsly's, a Bookseller at the sign of the Printing Press on the South Western Walk of the Royal Exchange."

Although the trial was not held with merchants as assessors, a merchant was, in fact, being asked to give his opinion on the custom of merchants before judgment was given. The court affirmed that the custom of merchants did not make any distinction between law and equity, and then general principles were laid down, which form the foundation of the law of merchants:

1. That every man's word should be as good as his deed.
2. That every creditor must have a debtor.
3. That everyone should answer for his own act or his own neglect whereby another is injured.

The particular technical problem which worried merchants was the time when foreign bills of exchange became due. Difficulties arose as a result of the old and new calendar, and it was decided that the time should be calculated by the calendar in use at the place where the bill was payable.

Roger North was one of the most vocal of Hale's critics, and his chief criticisms were that Hale was easily flattered, was vain and intolerant of opposition. His main objection was, however, political—that Hale was too partial to the popular party.

On the subject of vanity, North says: "It is most certain that his vanity was excessive; which grew out of a self-conversation, and being little abroad. But when he was off the seat of justice, and at home, his conversation was with none but flatterers."[3] It is true that he did not take part in social life and disliked social calls, especially in the morning. Nevertheless, we know that he dined frequently with Dr John Wilkins, and Richard Baxter often visited him at his home in Acton. Neither of these men can be regarded as flatterers. North admits that he was the most profound lawyer of his time, but adds: "he would be also a profound philosopher, naturalist, poet or divine", and thought himself as good in these subjects as in the law.[4] In fact, his interest in science was a recreation; he only wrote poetry on Christmas Day, and much of his writing on religious subjects was published without his consent. North is particularly scathing about his book *The Origination of Mankind* and this was certainly published during Hale's lifetime. This was a missionary book, written for unbelievers and atheists, and, although it can hardly be regarded as very persuasive, it is somewhat harsh to treat it as a sign of vanity. North maintains that Sir George Jeffries gained a great ascendancy over Hale in court by means of adroit flattery, but there is no means of testing this opinion. He suggests that a

good method of influencing Hale was to invite him to a meal in
private, when he could sit at ease and smoke his pipe, which he
much enjoyed.[5]

North grudgingly admits that Hale did justice to the King when
the law was on the King's side. "I have heard him [Francis North]
say that, while Hale was Chief Baron of the Exchequer, by means
of his great learning, even against his inclination, he did the
Crown more justice than any others in his place had done with
all their goodwill, and less knowledge. But he [Francis North]
knew also his foibles, which was leaning towards the popular;
yet, when he knew the law was for the King (as well he might,
being acquainted with all the records of the court, to which men
of law are commonly strangers), he failed not to judge accordingly."[6]

Nevertheless, North claims that Hale was prejudiced against
courtiers. "If one party was a courtier, and well dressed, and the
other a sort of puritan with a black cap and plain clothes, he
insensibly thought the justice of the cause was with the latter.
If the dissenting or anti-court party was at the back of a
cause, he was seldom impartial; and the loyalists had always a
great disadvantage before him."[7] It is certain that Hale's personal
predilections would be for the Puritan rather than the courtier,
but there is no evidence that this ever affected his judgments.

North maintained that his high reputation as a lawyer made
Hale intolerant of the opinion of others. "That judge had acquired
an authority so transcendant that his opinions were, by most
lawyers and others, thought incontestable; and he was habituated
in not bearing contradiction, and had no value for any person
whatever that did not subscribe to him."[8] Unfortunately there is
no means of testing this statement, but there may be an element
of truth in it. His opinions on matters of law were usually right,
and he may well have become intolerant of opposition especially
in his latter years, when he was known to the Norths.

Despite all his criticisms, North wrote favourably of Hale as a
lawyer. "He becomes the cushion exceedingly well; his manner
of hearing patient, his directions pertinent, and his discourses
copious, and although he hesitated, often fluent. His stop for a
word, by the produce, always paid for the delay; and, on some
occasions, he would utter sentences heroic."[9] Or again, "I have
known the Court of King's Bench sitting every day from 8 to 12,
the Lord Chief Justice Hale managing matters of law to all
imaginable advantage to the students, and in that he took
pleasure, or rather pride. He encouraged, arguing when it was to
the purpose, and used to debate with counsel, so that the court

might have been taken for an academy of sciences, as well as a seat of justice."[10] North refers to Hale's mannerism of putting his thumbs in his girdle, and in nearly every portrait, when his hands are shown, the thumb of one hand is stuck in the girdle.

North also had comments to make on Hale's family. "This great man was most unfortunate in his family; for he married his own servant maid, and then, for an excuse, said there was no wisdom below the girdle. All his sons died in the sink of lewdness and debauchery; and, if he was to blame in their education, it was by too much rigour, rather than of liberty; which [rigour] Montaigne says seldom fails of that consequence."[11] John Aubrey says that Hale was married for the first time in 1640, and that he was a great cuckold, and that in 1656 he married secondly the sevant maid Mary.[12]

Being a gossip, strict accuracy is not one of Aubrey's strong suits. Whether he was a cuckold or not we do not know, but with regard to his second marriage, this did not take place until 1667, and his second wife's name was Anne, not Mary. We have Baxter's evidence that the second wife was not in the same social class, and the family tradition is that Anne Bishop was his house-keeper.

With regard to the morals of his sons, although Hale made adequate provision for all his children, by means of settlements made *inter vivos*, he himself admits that his eldest son, Robert, died, leaving his children destitute and unprovided for.[13] Robert certainly died suddenly, under the age of 30 years, and his wife died a few months afterwards. In the preface to his letters to his grandchildren, he writes: "I have applied my counsels to them (my children), which while they followed, they did well, lived comfortably, and were a great comfort to me and to themselves, and when they have left and forsaken these counsels, they have miserably miscarried."[14] Although Hale had made proper pro-vision for his son, Edward, he clearly made advances to him, and in his will forgave him these debts.

Hale took a very gloomy view of the state of morality after the Restoration, and his views may have been coloured by personal experience with his sons. He writes: "It is rare to find a temperate or sober master, or a sober and faithful servant, a sober and dis-creet husband, or a prudent and modest wife."[15] He is very scathing about gentlemen who think it below them to do any work, or even look after their own estate, and also spend their time in feasting, drinking, gaming, wearing the latest fashions, go-ing to plays and balls, and paying social calls. "His estate is con-sumed and shuffled over into the hands of players, gamesters, vintners, tapsters, tailors, usurers and brokers, and in a little time, the gentleman hath nothing left to him but the title and many times ends his days in jail."[16]

Young gentlewomen do not come off any more lightly.

They make it their business to paint and patch their faces and curl their locks, and to find out the newest and costliest fashions. They do not arise before 10 o'clock, and the morning is spent between the comb and the glass and the box of patches. Although they cannot provide it themselves, they must have choice food prepared for them. When they are ready for the next business, they come down, and sit in the parlour which has been cleaned for them until Dinner time. After dinner, to cards or the exchange or a play, or to Hyde Park, or a social call. After supper, they go to a Ball or to cards. Their father's or husband's money is spent on costly clothes and entertainments, and they are never without company.[17]

In a few years or months, they have run through their husband's money. We do not know if these examples are taken from his own family, but if so, it is not surprising that for his second wife he chose his housekeeper.

It has not been possible to find the date and place of birth of any of Hale's children. Robert was born about 1643. He matriculated at St Edmund's Hall Oxford, on 14th November 1661, aged 18 years,[18] having been admitted as a student at Lincoln's Inn on 9th May 1661[19]

On 16th February 1662 Robert and his brother Matthew took over their father's chambers in Garden Court, Garden Row, Lincoln's Inn on payment of £60. They were permitted to continue at the university for another year on the usual terms.[20] Robert does not appear to have been called to the bar, although his brothers Matthew and Thomas were called in 1669.

Robert married Frances, daughter of Sir Francis Chock of Avington in Berkshire. On the occasion of their marriage, Hale entered into a marriage settlement dated 24th January 1665, entailing Alderley House and most of his land and Alderley on Robert and his heirs in tail, and on 21st September 1666 he settled more land on Robert.[21] Robert had five children, Matthew, Gabriel, Anne, Mary and Frances. He died suddenly on 28th July 1670 and was buried on 30th July 1670.[22] His wife died very shortly afterwards on 17th December 1670,[23] and Hale undertook the care and upbringing of their five children. All the letters said to be written by Hale to his children and grandchildren were, in fact, written to these five grandchildren, around 1673, when Hale was 64 years of age[24]

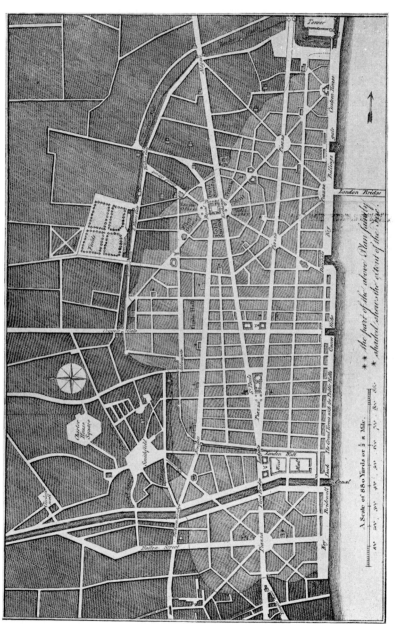

A plan of Sir Christopher Wren's proposed rebuilding of London after the Great Fire of 1666

(*left*) Richard Baxter,
friend of Matthew Hale

(*right*) John Wilkins,
Bishop of Chester

The second son Matthew was born about 1645. He also matriculated at St Edmund's Hall Oxford on 22nd May 1663, aged 18 years,[25] was admitted a student at Lincoln's Inn on 2nd January 1662 and was called to the bar on 27th October 1669.[26]

He married Anne, daughter of Matthew Simmonds of Hillesley, Gloucestershire, and died on 15th June 1675.[27] He had one son, Matthew, who was baptized at Alderley on 25th July 1676 after his father's death.[28] Hale also provided for his son by a settlement dated 12th October 1673 of the Manor of Rangeworthy, the Grange of Bagston and, by a settlement dated 18th January 1674, he settled other land in Rangeworthy, Thornbury, Week-warre, Bagston and Frampton Cotterell on his grandson, Matthew.[29]

The third son, Thomas, was born about 1647. He matriculated at St Edmund's Hall on 22nd May 1663, aged 16 years,[30] and was admitted a student at Lincoln's Inn on 11th March 1663. He was called to the bar on the same day as his brother Matthew, 27th October 1669.[31] He married Rebecca, daughter of Christian Le Brune, and on the occasion of their marriage on 15th December 1675, Hale settled on his son mills at Ewelme and land in Acton, Middlesex.[32] There was no issue of the marriage, and Thomas died about May 1676.

The fourth son, Edward, was born about 1649. There is no evidence that he went to Oxford, or that he was called to the bar. He married Mary, the daughter of Edmund Goodyere of Heythorp in Oxfordshire, and it is said that he had two sons and three daughters before he died in 1682. Hale made a marriage settlement on 2nd August 1674, settling land in Ewelme, Oxfordshire on Edward for life, with remainder to Mary his wife for life, and to Robert their son in tail male. This settlement appears to have been made after the marriage, as it specifically refers to Edward's son, Robert.[33] Edward was in the habit of obtaining advances from his father, as in the codicil to his will he forgave his son all debts due to him.

Hale's elder daughter, Mary, who survived him, married twice, firstly Edward Adderley of Innishannon, County Cork at Alderley on 25th July 1661.[34] They are said to have had two sons and three daughters, and certainly there was a son named Matthew who was baptized at Alderley on 12th April 1663. In his will, Hale gave £100 each to his grandchildren, Mary, Anne and Susan, and £200 to his grandson, Edward Adderley.[35] On the occasion of their marriage, Hale settled on Mary the house where he was born, Alderley Grange, and other lands in Alderley. He subse-

H

quently settled on her land in Old Sodbury, Little Sodbury and Chipping Sodbury.[36]

Mary married secondly Edward Stephens of Cherington, Gloucestershire, and the parish records of Alderley show that three children were baptized there: Elizabeth on 13th April 1678, Esther on 18th August 1680 and John on 17th July 1689.

The younger daughter, Elizabeth, married Edward Webb, a barrister-at-law, at Alderley on 31st January 1665.[37] The Webbs were a very old established family in Alderley, and the name appears frequently in the records. They had two children, Elizabeth and Edward, who received legacies of £10 each under Hale's will. There is no mention of a settlement on her marriage, and it can be assumed that her husband was a man of means.

Burnet says that Hale had ten children, but that four died in infancy. There is no evidence of this. Anne Moore was born in 1621 and, if the marriage took place in 1642, would only be 21 years of age. Robert, the eldest son, was born in 1643, and it is most unlikely that she would have had four children before the age of 21 years, all of whom died in infancy.

Hale, throughout his time on the Bench, kept the goodwill and respect of the King, but he was not popular with courtiers and men like Roger North. The main reason for this is that he did not support the persecution of Dissenters, Presbyterians and Quakers. On 1st December 1672 the Committee on Foreign Affairs decided in secret that Sir John Archer of the Court of Common Pleas and Hale should be removed after the Parliamentary session had expired.[38] Archer was, in fact, removed and replaced by Sir William Ellis. Hale retained his appointment, presumably because the King would not hear of his removal.

NOTES

1 Modern Reports, p. 74 .
2 On a trial before Lord Chief Justice Hale between Nathaniel and John Letten and Leonar Moresco, London, 1671.
3 Robert North, *The Lives of Francis North, Dudley North and John North*, vol. I, p. 121.
4 ibid., p. 121.
5 ibid., p. 124.
6 ibid., p. 119.
7 ibid., p. 119.
8 ibid., p. 118.
9 ibid., p. 120.
10 ibid., p. 139.
11 ibid., p. 124.

12 John Aubrey, *Brief Lives*.
13 Letters to his grandchildren, preface, B. M. Harl MS. 4009.
14 ibid.
15 ibid.
16 ibid., ch. 14.
17 ibid., ch. 16.
18 Joseph Foster, *Alumni Oxoniensis 1500–1714*, vol. II.
19 Admission book, Lincoln's Inn.
20 ibid.
21 Hale's will: J. B. Williams, *Life of Hale*, p. 327.
22 Alderley parish registers.
23 ibid.
24 Letters to his grandchildren, preface, B. M. Harl, MS. 4009.
25 Joseph Foster, *Alumni Oxoniensis 1500–1714*, vol. II.
26 Admission book, Lincoln's Inn.
27 Alderley parish register.
28 ibid.
29 Hale's will, J. B. Williams, *Life of Hale*, p. 327.
30 Joseph Foster, *Alumni Oxoniensis 1500–1714*, vol. II.
31 Admission book, Lincoln's Inn.
32 J. B. Williams, *Life of Hale*, p. 327.
33 ibid.
34 Alderley parish registers.
35 J. B. Williams, *Life of Hale*, p. 327.
36 ibid.
37 Alderley parish registers.
38 Alfred F. Havinghurst, "The Judiciary in the Reign of Charles II", *Law Quarterly Review*, 1950, vol. 66, p. 62.

XII

Last Days 1676

Hale remained in reasonably good health until late in 1675. His theory had always been that good health was to be used for his daily business and works of charity in the same way that good clothes were for use and not to be put away in a drawer for fear of wearing out. On the other hand he shunned places of infection, when there was no duty to go there, and unnecessary journeys. Overeating and overdrinking were also dangers which should be avoided.

He suffered at one time from stone, favouring pond water as a remedy in preference to gravel spring water, and stone may have been one of the contributory causes of his death. In October 1675 he suffered what was probably a severe and sudden coronary thrombosis from which he never fully recovered. Heart trouble prevented him from lying down, and he had to be propped in bed. Contemporaries spoke of him as having asthma, and this was clearly cardiac asthma with shortness of breath. He had a great interest in medicine and discussed his own symptoms and treatment with his physicians.

In the British Museum there is a manuscript in Hale's own hand, setting out the symptoms of his illness in great detail.[1] In health he had had eight hours sleep, but in his illness this was reduced to five hours. North-easterly winds made him short of breath, and moist, rainy and misty weather hindered sleep. He explains how different doctors had prescribed differently and there had been no correct diagnosis. "Some give it the common title which is now used in all illnesses which are not well understood, namely the scurvy. Others say it is dropsy—others not a true dropsy, but like a dropsy—others that it is asthma."

In October 1675 he travelled from Acton to Alderley, about 80 miles, and on his arrival he found his legs very swollen with what he himself thought was water. On 24th October he had great pain in both arms, chest and stomach, which lasted for two days. He

did not approve of blood letting, particularly in view of his age,
but 6 ounces of blood were taken, which relieved the pain. About
a week after this, he became so short of breath that he could
not lie down in bed, and one night it was so bad that he thought
he was going to die. At this crisis at twelve midnight he sent out
for a barber who took 6 or 7 ounces of blood, and this eased his
breathing.

Hale was absent from the court at the beginning of the Michaelmas Term 1675 in November as in one case it is stated that
he was sick.[2] A little later on in the term it is stated "Hale in
court",[3] so he clearly returned to London before Christmas,
although not taking any very active part in the business of the
court.

He resolved to retire as he was so weak that he could only
get to his seat in Westminster Hall with the help of his servants.
Many of his friends and acquaintances tried to dissuade him, but
in January 1676 he applied for a writ of ease. The King was loath
to grant his application, and urged him to do what he could in
his chambers. It was clear to Hale, however, that he could not do
the work and must retire. The King, although he could not refuse
the request, delayed making a decision, and the Lord Chancellor
refused to press the King despite the urgent requests of Hale.
Hale was now growing desperate on account of his weakness, and
it is reported that, on Sunday, 20th February 1676, he surrendered
his patent to the King, at the lodging of the King's Secretary,
Lord Coventry.[4] On 21st February he attended before a Master
in Chancery with a deed drawn by himself which he executed in
the presence of the Master and delivered it for enrollment. The
deed read as follows:

> To all persons in Christ whom these presents shall come. Matthew
> Hale, Knight, Chief Justice of our Lord, the King, assigned to hold
> pleas before the King, greeting: Know ye that I the said Matthew
> Hale, Knight, having now become advanced in years, and by reason
> of my age being now severely afflicted with various diseases and
> infirmities, and still confused thereby, do by this instrument resign
> and render to our most gracious Lord Charles the Second, by the
> Grace of God of England, Scotland, France and Ireland, King,
> Defender of the Faith, etc. the said office of Chief Justice; most
> humbly beseeching that this deed may be enrolled. In witness where-
> of I have set my seal to this deed of my resignation. Granted the
> 21st day of February in the twenty-eighth year of the reign of our
> said Lord the King.

He subsequently attended the Lord Chancellor and told him
that he had made the deed to show the world that he was retiring

freely and voluntarily and also to obviate any doubts which might arise from the question whether the Chief Justiceship was held at the King's pleasure or not.

He was received very kindly by the King, assuring him that he would look upon him as one of his judges and seek his advice when his health permitted. He also said that he would pay him his pension during his lifetime. Hale thought this was a bad precedent, and wrote to the Lord Chancellor, suggesting that the pension should be paid only during the King's pleasure, but the King would not hear of it. The original Deed of Grant of the annuity was dated 9th March 1675 and is in the possession of the Records Office at Gloucester. The annuity was £1,000 per annum payable quarterly on the Feast of the Annunciation of the Virgin Mary, the Nativity of St John the Baptist, the Feast of St Michael the Archangel and on the Nativity of our Lord, the first payment being made on the Feast of the Annunciation. The payment was expressed to be made "for and during the term of his natural life".

The question of whether a judge's appointment was "during pleasure" or "during good behaviour" was a live issue at the time and in Hale's view "during pleasure" was the law. In the Tudor period there was no uniform practice. The Barons of the Exchequer since the time of Henry VII held office during good behaviour, while the remainder held during pleasure. Under the Stuarts the Barons of the Exchequer held during pleasure and in 1641 Charles I declared his intention of appointing all judges during good behaviour, but no statute was passed to give effect to this intention.[5]

Hale had scruples about receiving an annuity for his life, and delayed applying for the pension for a month. When it was eventually received a large part was given away to charity. Hale's attitude to money has already been dealt with, but there is an anecdote told about him that, when he received bad money, he did not put it back in circulation, and consequently acquired quite a pile of bad coins. Thieves broke into his house, and got away with a very good haul, all of which were bad coins.

Before leaving London, he bade farewell to his servants, giving them all a token or memento, and giving some of them who had been with him a long time substantial cash gifts. His treatment of his servants was considerate and fair, but he always got rid of those who were immoral or unruly. His servants were always promoted strictly in accordance with seniority, as he held that it caused jealousy to promote a young man above the head of an older servant.

He cannot have been very popular with the court officials who had perquisites of office, as he made them share with the lower officials who only had their wages. It would be interesting to know how this was done whether by moral pressure only, or what sanctions there were to enforce such directions.

After his retirement Hale lived in his country home, Alderley House, where he spent the remaining months of his life. In February 1676 his legs, thighs and ankles became swollen, and he lost strength in his legs. He could not go upstairs or walk without falling. The flesh on his body became wasted, especially the upper part, and he had a great craving for coolness, avoiding heat and hot drinks. He lost weight and for six months slept propped up in bed. During all this time, his appetite remained good, his pulse and temperature normal, he had no headaches, his speech was clear and his mental faculties and memory alert.[6] He spent as much time as he could in his study, writing and revising the book *The primitive origination of mankind considered and examined according to the light of nature*. The book was published in the year after his death, in 1677.

Hale lived well within his income, and any surplus income was invested in the purchase of land. By 1676 he had acquired land in Gloucestershire, Oxfordshire, Staffordshire, Middlesex and Lincolnshire, although his most extensive estates were in Gloucestershire. He made provision for all his children by way of settlements of land made in his lifetime. Burnet says that he was a good landlord, always willing to reduce rent for a good reason. On one occasion, a widow who lived near him at Alderley complained that her rent was not being properly collected, so Hale arranged for his steward to act for her without payment. Later on, it became necessary to accept a reduced rent from her tenants, but Hale accounted to her for the full rent she should have received.

He had very humane views on the treatment of animals, holding that men had a duty towards animals and that it was wrong to treat them with cruelty or to kill them solely for the purposes of sport. Burnet gives some examples of his behaviour to animals. When his horses became too old for their work, he gave orders they were to be put out to grass, or given light work. On one occasion a shepherd had an old dog which had become blind, and he wanted to have him put down. Hale had the dog cared for in his own household. On another occasion he was very angry with a servant who neglected a bird so that it died of hunger. In his book *Contemplations Moral and Divine*, 1st ed., 1676, on p. 242 his views are clearly set out:

I have ever thought that there was a certain degree of justice due from man to the creatures as from man to man, and that an excessive, immoderate, unreasonable use of the creature's labour is an in-

120 MATTHEW HALE

justice for which he must account; to deny domestic creatures their
convenient food; to expect that labour from them that they are not
able to perform; to use extremity or cruelty towards them is a
breach of the trust under which the dominion of the creatures was
committed to us, and a breach of that justice that is due from men
to them; and therefore I have always esteemed it, as part of my
duty, and it hath been always my practice to be merciful to beasts.
Prov. 12.10. And upon the same account, I have ever esteemed it
a breach of trust, and have accordingly declined any cruelty to any
of thy creatures, and as much as I might, prevented it in others, as
a tyranny inconsistent with the trust and stewardship thou has committed to me. I have abhorred the sports that consist in the torturing
of creatures and if either noxious creatures must be destroyed, or
creatures for food must be taken, it hath been my practice to do it
in that manner that may be with the least torture or cruelty to the
creature. I have still thought it an unlawful thing to destroy those
creatures for recreation's sake that either were not hurtful when
they lived, or are more profitable when they are killed; ever re-
membering that thou has given us a dominion over thy creatures;
yet it is under a law of justice, prudence, and moderation otherwise
we shall become tyrants, not lords over thy creatures; and therefore those things of this nature that others have practised as
recreations I have avoided as sins.

Hunting is not absolutely prohibited. "I do think it lawful to
take the beasts that are useful for the food of man, that cannot be
taken otherwise than by hunting, as the stag, the buck, the doe, and
wild boar, but touching pursuing the harmless hare, one of the
most innocent of all beasts, and for no other end than for the sport
of it, with the possibility she is delivered up to the maws of the
hungry hounds, I could never approve, nor would since I came to
discretion."[7]

He goes on to consider the practical objections to hunting:

1. The cost of keeping hounds.
2. The time wasted in visits from the huntsman.
3. Giving offence to your poorer neighbours, by breaking down their
   fences, and riding over grass and corn.
4. Drinking afterwards.

Hale is constantly harking back to the evils of excessive drinking. In one of his letters to his grandchildren, he says: "The Common recreation now most in fashion is drinking, which is a brutish
and beastly recreation."[8] There are, in fact, very few recreations
which meet with his approval. The important thing is to avoid
recreations which are costly and entail a lot of time. Stage plays
are forbidden on account of the time spent, and all games of dice
are forbidden, as so many men are ruined, by this indulgence. It is

better not to play cards or gamble, but gambling is permitted, provided that you never play for more than you would freely give to the next poor man you meet. Chess is an ingenious and harmless game, but because it takes up a great deal of time, should only be played once a fortnight for two or three hours. The only recreation which meets with full approval is bowling, which is good and healthy exercise, but even here he thinks it should be limited to two to three hours. On no account should one visit a public bowling alley.

Hade made his last will on 3rd February 1675, before the onset of his illness, and added a codicil on 2nd November 1676 just before his death.[9] The will itself was clearly drafted by Hale personally, as it is characteristic in its completeness and attention to detail. He expressed the desire to be buried in the churchyard at Alderley on the south side of the tomb of his first wife. He gave directions for a marble gravestone with the inscription of his name only on it, and that his funeral should be private without any pomp, the whole not to cost more than £100. He says that he has made many settlements of his property on his family during his lifetime, but recites them all to avoid mistakes.

After giving legacies to various relatives, friends and servants, he gave £200 to his wife to be paid to her immediately on his death, and also gave to his wife "all my rings, clocks, watches, jewells, apparell, plate, brasse, pewter, lynnen, woollen, wheresoever and all my hangings, beds, and household stuffe in my said house at Alderley".

Apart from land, the main asset in his estate consisted of his library, and he gave to his wife "all those printed books of divinity, chyrugery, phisick, or history in English", which he would sign as evidence that these books were intended for her. He gave to his grandson Gabriel in the event of him studying law all his law reports and statutes, which he enumerated in detail. The most valuable of his manuscripts and books which he said he had been collecting for forty years, he gave to the Honourable Society of Lincoln's Inn, and specified them in detail in a schedule to his will. These manuscripts are still in the Library of Lincoln's Inn.

It is commonly thought that only members of Lincoln's Inn are at liberty to study these manuscripts, and the extract from Hale's will relating to the use of the book presented to Lincoln's Inn reads as follows:

As a testimony of my honour and respect to the Society of Lincoln's Inn, where I had the greatest of my education, I give and bequeath to the Honourable Society the several manuscript books in the schedule attached to my will. They are a treasure worth having and keeping, which I have been near 40 years in gathering with great industry and expense. My desire is that they be kept safe, and all together in remembrance of me. They were fit to be bound in leather, and chained and kept in archives. I desire that they may not be lent out or disposed of only if it happen hereafter to have any of my posterity of that Society that desire to transcribe any book and give very good caution to restore it again in a prefixt time such as the Benchers of that Society in Council shall approve of: then, and not otherwise, only one book at a time may be lent out to them, by the Society, so that there be no more than one book abroad out of the library at one time. They are a treasure that are not fit for every man's view; nor is every man capable of making use of them: only I would have nothing of these books printed but entirely preserved together for the industrious learned members of that Society.

He directed that he would have none of his manuscripts published save only those which he had expressly authorised in his lifetime. Apparently there was some licensing system in force before his death, which meant that certain parts of his manuscripts might have been edited and altered. This he disapproved of most strongly especially where law books were concerned.

In his codicil, dated the 2nd November 1666, he appears to have modified his views as he directed that if any of his books should be published the proceeds of sale should be divided into ten shares which he bequeathed as to seven shares to his servants and three shares to those who copied the manuscripts, and prepared them for publication. He appears to have left the decision about publication to the discretion of his executors. Most of his books were published by Thomas Shrewsbury, an Alderley man.

He appointed his wife, Sir Robert Jenkinson Bt, and Robert Gibbon of the Middle Temple to be his executors. Gibbon is described as "my servant", but he must have been a confidential secretary of some standing. There is at the Record Office at Gloucester a statement of account of provisions supplied to Hale in London, and the receipt is witnessed by Gibbon, so he clearly had charge of the housekeeping. It is from him that Burnet obtained much of the personal detail for his life of Hale. Sir Robert Jenkinson was an old friend.

He gave careful directions that his three granddaughters, Anne, Mary and Frances, should live with and be in the care of his wife, and that the two grandsons, Matthew and Gabriel, should live with his wife until such time as they should be sent away to school or university. He directed that the boys should be sent to school, but Matthew the eldest was not strong and should only be taught what he could assimilate. The younger boy, Gabriel, should have a more exacting education, so that he could take up the profession of the law if he had any aptitude or learning for it.

Hale occupied his time in reading and writing right up to the end, and although the pain increased, he maintained his faculties up to the end.

As the winter of 1676 approached, he became weaker and he had a premonition that he would die either on 25th November or on Christmas day. On the Sunday before he died, the vicar of Alderley, the Reverend Evan Griffiths suggested that he should bring the sacrament to Hale's house, but Hale insisted on being carried to the church to receive his communion in the usual way. He died peacefully on Christmas Day 1676 and was buried on 4th January 1677 in the churchyard of Alderley Church, as he did not approve of burials in churches, saying that churches were for the living and churchyards for the dead.

Besides his tombstone in Alderley churchyard, the only other memorial of him at Alderley is the church clock, which he presented to the church on the occasion of his sixty-fourth birthday.

When the clock was inspected in 1833, a paper was found on which the following words were printed: "This is the gift of the Right Honourable Chief Justice Hale to the Parish of Alderley. John Mason, Bristol, fecit 1. November 1673."[10]

NOTES

1 B.M. Stowe MS. 745, f.117.
2 Nellthorpe *v.* Farrington, Levinz Reports, pt. II, p. 113.
3 Bernardston *v.* Some, Levinz Report, pt. II, p. 114.
4 Keble Reports, vol. II, p. 622.
5 Alfred F. Havingsurst, "The judiciary in the reign of Charles II", *Law Quarterly Review*, 1950, vol. 66, p. 62.
6 B.M. Stowe MS. 745, f.117.
7 B.M. Harl MS. 4990, ch. 18, p. 81.
8 ibid., p. 79.
9 J. B. Williams, *Life of Hale*, p. 327.
10 J. M. Rigg, *Dictionary of National Biography*: Matthew Hale.

XIII

Books on Science
and Religion

1. *An essay touching the gravitation or non-gravitation of fluid
bodies and the reasons thereon.* London, 1673.

In his introduction Hale says that he is not satisfied with the
explanations given by others to the question of the gravity of
fluids. In his view men have formed theories and prejudiced the
issue and consequently may have rejected the truth. He states that
he had been giving a great deal of thought to the subject over the
years but the essay itself was written quickly. Characteristically
he states that although he naturally thinks his propositions are
true he may be wrong. The reason given for publication is that
better brains than his on this subject may read it and it may
stimulate them to reach the truth.

It is probable that Hale's interest in gravity arises out of his
interest in architecture and building. He considers pyramids, cones
and cylinders and explains certain experiments which he had
carried out. He took a cylinder of deal boards nailed together and
open at both ends 2 feet long by 6 inches diameter and two halves
of an empty egg shell. Clapped together the egg shell would not
stand a half-pound weight without being crushed. He put the egg
shell on a bed of fine sand and put the cylinder upon it. He then
gently poured sand into the cylinder up to the top. There was
about 4 pounds of sand in the cylinder and on top of that he put
a 6 or 7 pound weight of lead. Taking away the lead and sand
the egg shell was found to be intact. Hale attributed this to the
lateral pressure of the sand upon the sides of the cylinder whereby the minute particles of sand were driven to lean one on the
other and thus retained a kind of solidarity.

Hale had studied the books of Stevenius De Cartes and Mer-
senus and discusses their theories. His book contains a number of
diagrams to illustrate the questions discussed. It clearly has no

scientific value but it does illustrate his curiosity about natural phenomena and the truly scientific approach to the problems he was considering.

2. *Difficiles Nugae or Observations touching the Torricellian experiment and the various solutions of the same, especially touching the weight and elasticity of air.* London, 1674.

In the Torricellian experiment a glass tube of 3 feet or more is taken, closed at one end and filled with mercury or quicksilver. The open end is stopped with a finger and inverted in a vessel of mercury. When immersed the finger is taken away and the mercury in the tube will invariably subside by 27 to 30 inches leaving the upper part of the tube empty.

Hale's name is not given as the author on the ground that it would not be any advantage, and if his views are wrong it is easier for him to retract if his name is not known. He discusses the views of many men on the subject including Hobbes, Boyle and Pascall, and the book is mainly evidence of his wide reading on the subject of natural sciences.

This book and the previous one drew a reply by Dr Henry Moore entitled *Remarks upon two late ingenious discourses, the one an essay touching the gravitation and non-gravitation of fluid bodies and the other Observations touching the Torricellian experiment.* London, 1676.

3. *The primitive origination of mankind considered and examined according to the light of nature.* London, 1677.

After his retirement Hale spent some of his time revising this book, but ill health prevented him from revising it as thoroughly as he would have wished. He arranged for the manuscript to be sent to Wilkins for his opinion with no indication of the name of the writer except that the author was not a clergyman. Wilkins read it and sent it on to Tillotson, who guessed that the author must be Hale. They both went to see Hale to thank him for sending the manuscript to them, and Burnet says "he [Hale] blushed extremely, not without displeasure" thinking that the person who had sent the manuscript had given him away. Wilkins assured him that this was not the case and that they had guessed who the author was.

In this book Hale's conclusions were that, according to the light of nature and natural reason, the world was not eternal but had a beginning; that this truth is evident by reasons and arguments; that there is moral evidence of the truth of this assertion; that the mosaical system is consonant with reason.

In his preface he says that the reader may question why he should try to prove this truth as it is generally believed by Christians and that the book may create doubts rather than confirm belief. He replies that it is written for unbelievers and atheists and is therefore based on evidences of a natural and moral kind. The book was written over a long period of time and would not have been published but for the fact that *Contemplations Moral and Divine* had been published without his consent or knowledge. It was written "at leisure and broken times" when the pressure of other business permitted. He apologizes to the reader that his quotations from Aristotle, Plato, Plutarch and others are in Latin not Greek, "I was a better Grecian in the 16th than in the 66th year of my life and my application to another study and profession rendered my skill in that language of little use to me, so I wore it out by degrees." The book comprises 380 closely printed foolscap pages and illustrates well Hale's great failing of being too copious. It is closely reasoned but there is so much time spent on setting the scene, putting in the background and illustrating the points made that its sheer weight makes it unreadable.

4. *Liber secundus de Homines.*

This book was not published, but there is a manuscript in the British Museum (Add. MS. 9001). It concerns the secondary origination of mankind by natural propagation and contains 156 folio pages of manuscript. After some general remarks the book considers the propagation of vegetables and continues with the reproduction of animals and finally with man. It is interesting to note that those parts of the book which are not considered suitable for the young are written in Latin. He considers vegetables, flowers, trees, insects, mice and is constantly referring to the observations of Aristotle on the subject. The book shows his interest and knowledge of biology, physiology and medicine.

5. *Contemplations Moral and Divine,* London, 1676. (Also published by Thirlwall vol. II.)

Hale had suffered during his lifetime from unauthorized publication of his works and he was very sensitive to anything going out in his name which had not been revised and approved by him. It had been his practice on Sundays to set aside certain time for meditation, and with the object of fixing his thoughts and preventing his attention from wandering he had been in the habit of writing down his meditations. They were not intended for publication but for his own personal use. He refused to consent to their publication and they were in fact published without his consent or approval without any revision under the title *Contemplations Moral and Divine* on 3rd March 1676. This was done by a clergyman, the Reverend Anthony Saunders, a domestic chaplain to the Archbishop of Canterbury, who, thinking that it would be beneficial to the public to read the book considered that the end justified the means.

These meditations fill the whole of the second volume published by Thirlwall in 1805, but there are two chapters in particular which sum up a great deal of Hale's thinking on religion.

The first chapter deals with "The consideration of our latter end, and the benefits of it". If a man clearly faces the fact of his death many things which he thinks important are put in proper perspective. It makes life better and death easier. It makes a man more watchful, vigilant, industrious, cheerful and serviceable to God and other men.

The other chapter is about "The great audit with the account of the good steward". He stresses the law of accountability and that men have to account to God for the goods use of their talents, times and money.

6. *The judgement of the late Lord Chief Justice Matthew Hale on the nature of true religion the causes of its corruption and the church's calamity by men's additions and violence with the desired cure. In three discourses written by himself at different times.* Published by Richard Baxter, London, 1684.

This book contains Hale's views on the religious controversies of his time and was not intended for publication. During his last illness Baxter urged him to write his judgment on these controversies. After *Contemplations Moral and Divine* had been published the editor produced a bag of manuscripts and gave Baxter three saying that Hale had given directions for them to be handed to him. All three had been written long before at different times.

(a) The 1st Discourse relates to the ends and use of religion and how it is corrupted and changed in the world. He gave as his view: "The episcopal government constituted in England is the most excellent form of ecclesiastic government . . . and yet I do not think that the essence of the Christian religion consists in this or any other particular form of government." For example the Quakers; take away all the special trappings of Quakerism and they are found to be men as other men are, very sober, honest, just and plain-hearted and are true Christians.

He comments that men have a great partiality for their own ideas and opinions. A new fancy or opinion or a new form of worship is valued more highly by the man who invented it than an established form of religion. This is nothing more than the effect of self-love and self-conceit. "There is in most men a certain itch of pride which makes them like to be different and subdivide."

(b) The 2nd Discourse explains that the whole duty of man is to fear God and keep his commandments. Men are inclined to mix up religion with philosophy or State policy. There must be some rules but they should not be too numerous.

    (i) If there are too many rules they oppress rather than secure true religion.

    (ii) They must not be superstitious.

    (iii) Ceremonies should be decent but not too full of pomp and ostentation. "Ceremonies should be used as we use a glass, rather to preserve the oil than to adorn it."

    (iv) Not to adhere to ceremonies just because they are ancient.

    (v) Rules not to be urged with too much severity on those who cannot accept them for conscience's sake.

    (vi) Remember that religion is not comprised of ceremonies. They are the dressings and trimmings of religion but the reality lies in the fear of God.

"It is pitiful to see man make these mistakes; one placing all his religion in holding the Pope to be Christ's vice-regent; another placing religion in this to hold no papist can be saved . . . one holding a great part of religion in pulling off the hat, and bowing at the name of Jesus; another judging a man an idolator for it; and a third placing his religion in putting off his hat to no one; and so like a company of boys that blow bubbles out of a walnut shall every one run after his bubble and call it religion."

(c) The 3rd Discourse discusses the fact that the greatest heat and animosity in Christianity is engendered by the trappings and not by the substance of Christianity.

    (i) Men love the things which are their own and which they have created more than the things of God.

    (ii) Pride, credit and reputation are commonly engaged in both parties to a controversy which make differences irreconcilable. When differences occur gentleness, mildness and personal respect quiet the passions and gain a hearing. Seldom is any man converted and convinced by angry, passionate railing and personal vilification. His conclusion is that men for their own sakes and for the honour of the Christian religion should use temperance, prudence and moderation in controversies about non-essentials.

7. *A discourse of the knowledge of God and ourselves.* London, 1683.

 (i) By the light of nature.

(ii) By the sacred scriptures.

Sir Orlando Bridgeman, author of *Bridgeman's Conveyancer*

Alderley House (*above*) before its demolition in 1860 and (*below*) as depicted soon after Matthew Hale's death

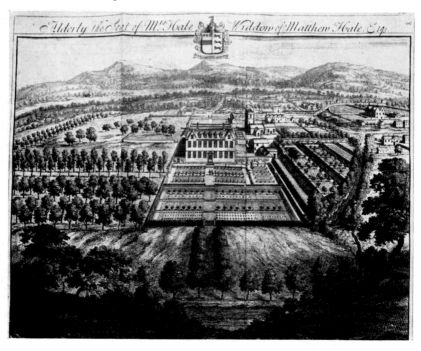

To which is added:
A brief abstract of the Christian religion (Thirlwall) vol. 1, p. 248
and
Considerations seasonable at all times for cleansing of the heart and
life (Thirlwall) vol. 1, p. 260, London 1683.

8. The following tracts have been published only by Thirlwall:
   A discourse on life and immortality, vol. I, p. 332.
   On the day of Pentecost, vol. I, p. 344.
   Concerning the works of God, vol. I, p. 366.
   Of doing as we would be done to, vol. I, p. 378.

XIV

Legal Writing

Burnet says that when Hale wrote he liked to prepare a plan in advance under various headings so that the subject could be treated in a systematic manner. Within this framework he wrote at length on each subject making sure that he had the background. In law in his time this meant looking back into the history of the subject to find the root of the matter. The judicial jurisdiction of the House of Lords could only be discovered by an historical survey and even a subject such as the methods of accounting adopted by sheriffs could only be explained by a study of what had happened in the past.

Hale wrote quickly and illegibly like someone whose speed of thought outstripped his manual dexterity, and he himself said that he had only to tap his thoughts and let them run.[1] Every question was debated fully and examined from every point of view and the results committed to paper.

When considering Hale's writings on law a warning is necessary with regard to the titles which are misleading for the modern reader. Hale's book *The History of the Pleas of the Crown* is not a history in the modern sense of the word. It is a textbook on criminal law dealing with crimes when punishment was death and the procedure in such cases. *The History of the Common Law* is only a few essays about certain aspects of the common law, and *The Black Book of the New Law* is Hale's abridgment of the laws of England.

There is frequently a duplication of subject matter and this is understandable when manuscripts were not intended for publication. For example, Chapters XVII to XX of *The History of the Pleas of the Crown* deal with coinage, whilst the same subject is touched on in *A Short Treatise Touching Sheriff's Accompts.* Chapter V of *The History of the Common Law* tells how William I came to the throne by way of succession and not conquest, and the same theory appears in his *Reflections on Hobbe's Dialogue of the law.*

His legal writings can be classified under four main headings:
For the Practitioner

1. *Summary of the Pleas of the Crown*
2. *The History of the Pleas of the Crown*
3. *The Black Book of the New Law*
4. *Notes on Fitzherbert's Natura Brevium*
5. *Notes on Coke's First Institute*

All these books except the *Black Book of the New Law* were published after his death and were the working notebooks of a practising lawyer built up over a lifetime.

Public Law

6. *The Jurisdiction of the Lord's House*
7. *Reflections on Hobbes' Dialogue of the Law*
8. *A Short Treatise on Sheriff's Accompts*
9. *A Treatise in Three Parts on the Customs*
10. *A Treatise on the Admiralty Jurisdiction*
11. *A Tract on the Law of Naturalisation*
12. *A Tract on the Court of Marches in Wales*
13. *A Tract on the Powers of the King*

All these manuscripts appear to have been written after the Restoration and are not scholarly studies in constitutional law but deal with the particular controversies that stirred he country at the time.

Law Reform

14. *The Analysis of the Law*
15. *Considerations Touching the Amendment and Alteration of Laws*
16. *Discourse Touching the Courts of King's Bench and Common Pleas*

Although Hale sat on the committee for law reform under the Commonwealth and drafted a number of bills his mature thoughts on the subject were written down after the Restoration.

Legal Education

17. *Preface to Rolle's Abridgment*
18. *The History of the Common Law*

The *Preface to Rolle's Abridgment* was specifically addressed to students, and it is suggested that *The History of the Common Law* may have been essays for students.

19. The manuscript of the *Law of Nature* does not fall into any

of the above categories as it is a hybrid, being partly legal and partly religious.

1. *Summary of the Pleas of the Crown*

The first authorised edition of this book was published in London in 1682 having been licensed for publication by Richard Raynsford J, on 18th March 1677. There had been a previous edition without the author being named (but commonly regarded as being by Hale). This was very full of inaccuracies. It had been transscribed by somebody unfamiliar with Hale's handwriting and his methods of work. He used to write paragraphs and then leave blank spaces which could be filled in when other material was found which fitted in. Sometimes these blank spaces got filled up and he would write what he wished to add on another sheet of paper without any proper system of references. The editor of the authorised edition worked hard to correct the mistakes and put the material in proper order.

The editor says in his preface that the book was written about the end of the reign of King Charles I or not many years after and was not intended for publication.[2] It was never revised and he says that Hale usually carried it with him on circuit. It was clearly a practitioner's notebook for ready reference and not a work of scholarship. It was the basis upon which the *History of the Pleas of the Crown* was built and the editor regards it as an introduction for students and a synopsis of the criminal law.[3]

The book went through seven editions, the sixth edition in 1754 and the last being in 1773, edited by G. Jacob. The summary forms the second part of Hale's *The Analysis of the Law*, that is the criminal law. It is confusing as what is published as *An Analysis of the Law* is the civil side only, and this book is an epitome of the criminal law.

2. *The History of the Pleas of the Crown*

This is undoubtedly the most important of Hale's works and is the result of a lifetime's study of the criminal law. In his preface Hale says that he intends to make a full collection of the Pleas of the Crown and to divide these pleas into two general headings, criminal and civil.[4] The first book will be divided into two sections, capital offences and procedure in capital offences. The second will deal with criminal offences which are not capital, and the third book will relate to franchises and liberties.[5] In fact only the first book was written and it is this book which is called *The History of the Pleas of the Crown*. It should be noted that Hale himself in his Proemium refers to making a full collection of the Pleas of the Crown.

The book was not published during Hale's lifetime, but on 29th November 1680 the House of Commons ordered that Hale's executors be desired to print the manuscript relating to Crown law and that a committee be appointed to supervise publication. The committee consisted of Sir Will Jones, Serjeant Maynard, Sir Francis Winnington, Mr Sacheverel, Mr George Pelham and Mr Paul Foley.[6] However, soon afterwards Parliament was dissolved and nothing was done.

The full text of *The History of the Pleas of the Crown* was not published until 1736, when the work of preparation for publication was undertaken by Sollom Emlyn. The editor says that he used the original manuscript in Hale's own handwriting. The original had been transcribed in Hale's lifetime and the transscript bound in seven small volumes in folio.[7] Hale had revised the manuscript as far as Chapter 27, approximately one quarter of the whole work.[8] These revisions are made in Hale's own hand and are voluminous. The editor did his work most thoroughly and checked the references with the original records and found that Hale had frequently copied from the misprinted quotation in the margin of Coke's *Third Volume of his Institutes*. He also found some of the references from year books, reports etc. had been quoted without folio or page number or else misquoted.[9]

The book was published in two volumes containing 710 folio pages of text. The first volume relates to the substantive law relating to capital offences. Nineteen chapters are devoted to treason, nine to murder and manslaughter, five to larceny and one to heresy and arson. There are chapters on arrests, accessories before and after the fact, rape, abduction of wife, purveyor taking victuals without warrant, and a description of the felonies created by statute from the time of Edward II to Charles II.

The second volume deals with the procedure relating to capital offences. The first seven chapters deal with the powers and jurisdiction of the Court of King's Bench, the Court of the High Steward, the various commissions of oyer and terminer, the powers of the judges of assize, coroners and sheriffs. Then the pursuit of the criminal is dealt with chronologically starting with arrests, Justices of the Peace, bail, warrant to search, indictments, certiorari, arraignment, pleas of prisoner, trial by jury, challenge, evidence and witnesses, verdict, benefit of clergy, judgment, execution and reprieve.

This book is a *tour de force*. It is systematic and detailed and a modern publisher would describe it as indispensable for any lawyer practising criminal law. It has always been judged as of the highest authority. Hale succeeded in reducing the mass of material to a coherent account of the criminal law relating to capital offences and it is one of the classic books of English Law.

3. *The Black Book of the New Law*

This book is in manuscript in Lincoln's Inn Library and is Hale's commonplace book or abridgment of the law. It is the original manuscript written in Hale's own handwriting in law French, containing 300 pages closely written on folio paper starting with abuttals, answer, accord, account and administration and ending with waifs and strays and watch and ward.

It is not possible to make any true assessment of the value of this book. The handwriting is very difficult to decipher, and although law French is easy to follow with a moderate knowledge of French it adds to the difficulties. We know that Hale himself regarded it as a book of the greatest value and he makes special mention of it in his will. It is a pity that it was not published in 1668 instead of Rolle's *Abridgment*. Hale was undoubtedly a better scholar than Rolle and also a man of wider legal experience, as Rolle's practice had been mainly in the Court of King's Bench. Burnet says that one of the other judges borrowed this book and was amazed at the learning it contained.

It is probably the most important source book for the law of the seventeenth century that exists, but it requires deciphering, translating and annotating. Owing to the length of the manuscript and the references to early statutes and documents it would be a tremendous task to edit.

4. *Notes upon Fitzherbert's New Natura Brevium*

Hale made notes in the margin of his copy of Fitzherbert which formed a commentary. This was published as *New Natura Brevium, with Sir Matthew Hale's Commentary*, London 1730. The eighth edition translated into English was published in 1755 and reprinted in 1794 in two octavo volumes. Fitzherbert's book is a discussion of the nature and purpose of original writs, and Hale appears to have concentrated on certain subjects which the editor specifies in the preface:

(a) To the Church and Churchmen
(b) To the regal state and government
(c) To real rights and estates in land and offices
(d) To personal rights in goods and chattels
(e) To the method of process and proceedings

Certainly the annotations are fuller on these subjects but whether this is intentional or not it is hard to say.

5. Notes on Coke's First Institute

Hale made notes on his copy of the *First Institute of the Laws of England or a Commentary upon Littleton's Tenures* by Sir Edward Coke. The fourteenth edition published in 1789 and edited by Francis Hargrave includes Hale's notes. It is recorded in the preface of this edition that the original manuscript notes by Hale were given by Hale to the father of Philip Gibbon. This would probably be Robert Gibbon, Hale's steward and executor. A copy was made for the use of Charles Yorke, then Solicitor-General, and Hargrave published from this copy.

6. The Jurisdiction of the Lord's House, or Parliament Considered According to Ancient Records

In 1657 there was general liberty to trade in the East Indies and Skinner sent a ship to the East Indies to trade. Agents of the East India Company at Bantan seized his ship and goods and arrested him at his warehouse at Jamba in Sumatra on the excuse that there was a debt due from him to the East India Company.

Negotiations for a settlement dragged on, Skinner claiming £3,300 and the highest figure offered by the company being £1,500. Skinner petitioned the House of Lords for relief and the matter was referred to the judges for their advice. The judges gave their opinion that the common law courts had jurisdiction in respect of offences committed by British nationals out of the jurisdiction.[10] This is probably how Hale first became involved in this question of the jurisdiction of the House of Lords.

Between 1667 and 1669 there was a great deal of controversy between the House of Lords and House of Commons on the subject of the original jurisdiction of the House of Lords in civil cases arising out of Skinner's case, the House of Lords claiming such a jurisdiction and the House of Commons disputing it. At the end of 1669 the King himself stepped in and suggested that the records of both Houses about the case be erased. This was accepted by both Houses. The House of Commons also refused to accept the claim of the House of Lords to have an appellate jurisdiction in Chancery.

In Hale's view the judicial power of Parliament was exercised by the king, the Lords and Commons in the same manner as the legislative power and was merely one facet of the same power. The judicial power of the king in Parliament was exercised through the *consilium ordinarium* (growing out of the *consilium regis*, it comprised the House of Lords sitting with the judges and officers of state and exercising judicial powers). The great officers of state, the judges and other members of the *consilium* were constitutionally entitled to a voice equally with the Lords. On the legislative side these great officers and the judges were merely assistants.

Hargrave says that Hale wrote two papers on the subject before this book was finally written. The first paper entitled "A discourse or history concerning the power of judicature in the King's Council and in Parliament" was written in 1669 when Hale was Chief Baron of the Exchequer and contains eleven chapters.[11] This was written on the occasion of the dispute between the two Houses in Skinner *v*. East India Company and disproved the pretension of the House of Lords to have any original jurisdiction.

A second paper entitled "Preparatory notes touching Parliamentary proceedings"[12] contains twenty-seven chapters and deals with the appellate jurisdiction of the House of Lords.

Hargrave says that the final work was contained in a manuscript in Hale's own handwriting except Chapter 30 and was based on the "Preparatory Notes". The handwriting shows that it was one of Hale's last works and he quotes a King's Bench case as late as 1673. The last few pages are barely legible and under the title is written "This book is perfected but I have not yet revised it after it was written. M.H."[13]

Hale formed the view that the House of Lords had no original jurisdiction in civil cases nor in criminal matters without impeachment by the House of Commons and this view was subsequently held to be the law.

He concluded that the House of Lords had at that time no appellate jurisdiction over causes in equity but this view did not prevail.

This book starts with a study of the *consilium regis*, its jurisdiction, its relationship to the Court of Chancery and the Court of King's Bench; continues with the nature of Parliamentary petitions and procedure; considers the jurisdiction of the House of Lords at first instance, in civil cases and criminal matters; considers appellate jurisdiction of the House of Lords and has a chapter on appeals from the Court of Chancery. Finally he makes certain recommendations. He suggests that the appointment of tryers of petitions made by the King on the first day of the session should not be a formality but that the King should select the most judicious peers who together with the judges should be commissioned under the Great Seal to hear petitions and that writs of error should be referred to this body. The judges would not only be assistants to advise the peers but commissioners in their own right. Hearing of appeals would not engage the whole House but a specially qualified committee of the House could undertake the work.[14]

Holdsworth says that this book is the most important of Hale's published works dealing with constitutional and public law.[15] It must be doubted, however, whether the book has any great importance as a treatise on constitutional law. It is Hale's arguments to support his views on the jurisdiction of the House of Lords which was one of the hotly debated questions of his time.

The importance of the book lies more in the conclusions reached than in the arguments and evidence on which these are based. His suggestions would, no doubt, be considered by those in authority and the idea of exercising the power of the House through a judicial committee was adopted and remains with us to this day. The book was an attempt to ascertain what the law was on this particular subject and to make suggestions for its improvement. Its object was to persuade. He could see no purpose in the House of Lords having any original jurisdiction as the Courts of Common Law and the Court of Chancery were better equipped to deal with matters in the first instance. There was, however, great value in keeping the jurisdiction of the House as a court of appeal and he made specific proposals aimed at improving the composition of the House for this purpose.

7. *Reflections on Hobbes' Dialogue of the Law*

According to Sir Frederick Pollock, Hobbes' *Dialogue on the Law* was not printed until 1681, and he says that down to the early part of the eighteenth century, if not even later, it was the common practice to circulate unpublished works among learned people who might be interested.[16] Hale would undoubtedly have had to read the manuscript to make this reply and it must have come to him in this way.

Holdsworth says that Hale had not really grasped Hobbes' theory of sovereignty.[17] Hobbes said: "In all cities or bodies politic not subordinate but independent, that one man or one council, to whom the particular members have given that common power, is called their sovereign, and his power the sovereign power; which consisteth in the power and strength that every of the members have transferred to him from themselves, by covenant."[18] Hale was quick to point out that this did not fit in with the constitutional position in his day and he set about refuting Hobbes' theories which he believed to be mischievous in the political circumstances of the time.[19] The original manuscript is lost but there are two copies in the British Museum. The text can be most conveniently found in the appendix to Holdsworth's *A History of English Law*, vol. V, p. 500.

The first part of the tract is taken up with an examination of the shortcomings of reason. Hale points out that it is common knowledge that some men are more apt in some subjects than in others. One man may exercise his faculty of reasoning to the best effect as a physician but would be useless as a politician. "Tully that was an excellent orator, and a great moralist, was but an ordinary stateman and a worse poet . . . commonly those that pretend to a universal knowledge are but superficial and seldom pierce deep into anything."[20] When a man has practised an art or science such as mathematics or law he is a better mathematician or lawyer than a man of equal intellect who has not had the practise and experience.[21] In fact there are certain subjects where a full knowledge of the subject must be present before reason can usefully be applied. In morals and politics it is seldom that men can agree however great their intellectual ability and he cites the disagreement between Plato and Aristotle on framing the laws and their commonwealth.[22]

Hale says that although law cannot cover every circumstance it is better that way than "the arbitrary and uncertain rule which men miscall reason".[23] He stresses the importance of law being certain but incurring the minimum of ill effects. It is extremely difficult to frame a law where the inconveniences are less than the benefits. A certain law may cause some to suffer yet far more would suffer if the law is arbitrary and uncertain. Hale says that "The texture of human affairs is not unlike the texture of a diseased body labouring under maladies, it may be of so various a nature that such physic as may be proper for the cure of one of the maladies may be destructive in relation to another, and the cure of one disease may be the death of the patient."[24] Nevertheless his view that the law should be certain in particular where rights of property and contract are concerned is shared by most English judges and jurists. "The inconvenience of an arbitrary is intolerable, and therefore a certain law though accompanied with some mischief is to be preferred. But it is not possible for any human thing to be wholly perfect."[25]

He says that there are many things in law which can reasonably be approved although the reason may not be apparent. For example it seems reasonable to him to prefer a law made by a hundred or two hundred men of experience to one made by himself. He can fully understand the one made by himself but may not understand the one made by the others. Again he thinks it reasonable to prefer a law by which the kingdom has been happily governed for 400 years to some new theory of his own, however reasonable it may be. "Long experience makes more discoveries touching conveniences or inconveniences of laws than is possible for the wisest council of men at first to foresee. And that those amendments that through the various experiences of wise and knowing men have been applied to any law must needs be better suited to the convenience of laws than the best inventions of the most pregnant wits."[26]

He further claims that law is a settled institution and that it is not necessary that we should know the reason why, for example, land passed to the eldest son. It is sufficient that law is certain and settled, although the reason is not apparent. It is vain to speculate how the law of primogeniture came about as laws of this nature were introduced by custom and usage or by Act of Parliament. Men are not born common lawyers and cannot become so merely by the exercise of reason but only by study and experience.[27] Although a man who has studied the law cannot be infallible he is much better fitted to make legal judgments than one who has not. He stresses again the need for the law to be certain, and if this is to be so lawyers must have a good knowledge of the law, Acts of Parliament and decisions of the judges. This was particularly important in the exposition of Acts of Parliament as they would know better what judges had said about the Act and how similar Acts of Parliament had been put into operation.

The second part of the manuscript dealt specifically with "sovereign power", and he describes the various methods by which the powers of government can be acquired:

(a) By consent of governor and governed but he admits that it is difficult to trace any such government owing to the changes occasioned by time.

(b) By long usage and custom with the implication of the consent of governor and governed.

(c) By conquest. Absolute conquest is rare and usually there is a capitulation agreement. He then digresses into a discussion of the Norman Conquest. According to him, William did not conquer England and abrogate all former laws and customs. The claim of William was not by right of conquest but of succession to King Edward and on these grounds Harold was the usurper. There was no general alteration of the law of property and men held their land in the same way as before. This was a theory which he expounded in more detail in Chapter V of his *History of the Common Law*.

He sets out the threefold effect of the law of England or any other country:

(a) Potestus Coerciva. Extends to all subjects but king is not subject to the coercive power of the law.

(b) Potestus Directiva. The king is bound by the solemn oath taken

at his coronation confirming the Great Charter and those other
laws affecting the liberty of the subject.

(c) Potestus Irritans. The king must act in accordance with law in
many specific instances. For example, grants of land must be
under the Great Seal and grants of monopolies are void.[28]

He then examines the powers which the king only can wield:

(a) The power of declaring war and making peace.
(b) Coining money.
(c) Reprieve, or pardoning public offences.
(d) From him derives all powers to administer justice.
(e) Power to raise the militia and armed forces at land and sea—
although this is subject to two limitations, that no man can be
forced to serve out of the kingdom and that no taxes can be
imposed for military purposes without the consent of Parliament.
(f) Power to make laws, although laws cannot be made without the
advice and consent of both Houses of Parliament.[29]

Yet despite these facts, he says "there are certain speculators
that take upon them to correct all Governments in the world and
to govern them by certain notions and fancies of their own and are
transported with so great confidence and opinion of them that they
think all States and Kingdoms and Governments must presently
conform to them".[30]

These notions are that there can be no qualification to the power
of the sovereign and that he can repeal and alter laws, impose
taxes and take the property of his subjects as he please. Louis XIV
of France certainly thought of himself in these terms as an absolute and sovereign power. So far as England is concerned Hale
treats these "wild propositions" as being (a) utterly false, (b) against
all natural justice, (c) pernicious to government, (d) destructive
of the common good and safety of the government, (e) without
any shadow of law or reason to support them.[31]

They are false because the laws and customs of the kingdom are
facts which exist. It is certain that the king cannot make a binding
law without the consent of the Lords and Commons in Parliament,
neither can he repeal a law without such consent. They are against
natural justice as the king as well as his subjects is bound to keep
faith and promises, particularly the solemn oath made at his
coronation to observe and keep the laws of the land and the liberties of the subject.[32] They are pernicious to government as it is
vital to good government that there should be confidence between
governor and governed and there can be no such confidence when
the governor can abrogate and suspend the rights and liberties of
the governed at his will. What could be more pernicious than to
tell the world that the government is not bound to keep the laws

that he and his ancestors have made with the consent of Parliament and that he may repeal such laws as he thinks fit. "Such a man that teacheth such a doctrine as this as much weakens the Sovereign Power as is imaginable and betrays it with a kiss."[33] The governed are apprehensive about what will happen to their property. Initiative is stifled and enterprise damped down.[34] It is in the interest of the government to use its power for the benefit of the governed, to keep them rich and consequently obedient rather than poor and desperate.[35] "Yet it is most certain that if once men be under that jealousy that the laws of the land do not sufficiently fix their properties and liberties men's minds will be pendulous and unquiet and subject to fears and doubts, and thereupon industry will wither and decay, whatsoever orations men of wit and eloquence may otherwise make to secure them."[36]

8. A Short Treatise Touching Sheriffs Accompts

A dispute arose between the Auditors of the Revenue and the Clerks of the Pipe, the Auditors claiming that the Clerks of the Pipe had a deficiency in their accounts and the Clerks of the Pipe denying this. The matter was referred by the Lord High Treasurer and Chancellor of the Exchequer to Hale and this treatise is in fact his judgment on the controversy.

The treatise was dedicated to the Lord High Treasurer and the Chancellor of the Exchequer and in his introduction he says that it has not been easy for him to check all the facts as many of his papers are in London and "I fear, hardly to be retrieved into a due order in regard to the late distraction."[37] It was clearly written after 1660, when Hale was Chief Baron of the Exchequer, although the exact year is not known, and is quite short, about 16,000 words.

The book begins with a consideration of the weight of silver and he explains the difference between rents numero, i.e. paid in pounds troy weight, and rents blanc, i.e. paid in purest silver tried in fire. At first the king's rents were paid in numero but later in blanc to avoid counterfeiting. One of the functions of the sheriff was to act as the king's bailiff, to collect his revenue in the county, improving and letting the king's land and collecting his rents. With regard to rents these were of two kinds: fixed rents, such as rents received by the king direct from the tenants of his lands, and casual rents. The latter consisted of fees payable to the king for litigation in county courts and hundred courts. Hale describes in detail all the sources of the king's revenue which it was the duty of the sheriff to collect.

The sheriff had to account twice yearly at Easter and Michael-

mas, and just before Easter and Michaelmas[38] a writ was issued out
of the Exchequer called the Summons of the Pipe, which had an-
nexed to it a schedule of the rents and sums payable to the king
under the different categories. These were not however particular-
ised to show exactly what was charged on each particular piece of
land. The sheriff was charged with all the rents set out in the
summons, but in course of time many rents were sold or became
worthless. This was a cause of complaint by sheriffs over a long
period of time that the Summons of the Pipe did not show the true
position and that they were charged with rents which could not be
collected. By a statute of 34 Henry VIII cap. 16[39] sheriffs were
given allowances for expenses such as entertaining justices and
many of them used this power to good purpose to the detriment
of the Crown.

The Clerks of the Pipe were cleared by Hale as, although they
used different methods of accounting from the Auditors of the
Revenue, there were no deficiencies in their accounts.[40] It was
merely that the auditors did not understand all the technicalities
which had grown up over a long period of time. Hale also decided
one or two minor points on the accounts.

Hale makes some suggestions for reform:

(a) He points out the inconvenience of using a method of account-
    ing established in the time of King Stephen and recommends
    that the methods used by the Auditors of the Revenue should
    be adopted as being more intelligible and better suited to the
    times.[41]
(b) That small rents should be redeemed for a capital sum by the
    townships and persons charged with them.[42] These were not
    worth the trouble and expense of collection.
(c) When sums are due to a sheriff from the king it was the practice
    to set it off against any debt due by the sheriff or any other
    sheriff. Hale suggests that although this worked in practice it
    would be well that such allowances should not be made without
    a warrant from the Lord Treasurer or order of the court and a
    memorandum endorsed on the roll that the debt had been dis-
    charged in this way.[43]

9. *Treatise on Rivers, the Foreshore, Ports and Customs*

This is one of Hale's writings published in Hargrave's *Tracts*,
vol. 1, p. 1, in three parts, and there is a manuscript copy in the
British Museum Add. MSS. 30228 entitled *Treatise on Maritime
Law*.

The first part relates to the rights of the king and the public in
rivers and the sea and foreshore and the prerogative and franchise
with regard to wrecks. The second part deals with ports, the rights

of the king and the public to enter ports and the rights of the king in relation to trade and customs. The third part concerns customs and the customary duties the king is entitled to levy. There are nine chapters devoted to the history of customs since the time of Edward I, followed by a discussion of duties payable by aliens and the privileges of the Hanseatic merchants, when customs are due and when not due, entry of goods inwards and outwards and how made, definitions of shipping and unshipping, concerning the time and place of loading and unloading goods, repayment of customs, special duties such as customs on Newcastle coal and on cloth.

Chapter XVI deals with the customs in the time of Charles II so it appears that the work was written after the Restoration when Hale was Chief Baron of the Exchequer. Hargrave says that the object of the author was to give a legal history of the customs from their earliest infancy to the Restoration and for some few years after. He suggests that the first and second parts were preliminary and introductive.[44] The main purpose of the treatise was certainly a discussion of the customs, but it was not intended as legal history. Customs and taxation were an important subject of controversy in the time of Charles II and, as Chief Baron of the Exchequer, points of law would frequently be referred to Hale. It is probable that the treatise was written at the request of the Chancellor of the Exchequer in the same way as *Sheriffs' Accompts*, but we do not know for certain the purpose for which it was written.

10. *A Treatise on the Admiralty Jurisdiction*

There are two identical manuscripts on this subject in the British Museum.[45] The treatise is entitled *A disquisition touching the jurisdiction of the Common Law and Court of Admiralty in relation to things done upon or beyond the sea touching maritime and merchants contracts.*

In his introduction he writes that that law is best that is best for the people whose law it is as the shell of an oyster is better for an oyster than a shell of a periwinkle or scallop though this may look finer and be fitter for that fish whose shell it is.[46] Many countries are unwilling to admit the civil law as having rid themselves of the Roman Empire think it would be a kind of recognition or badge of servitude to recognize it. In England civil law has never had any great acceptance in point of jurisdiction and cannot be exercised as a rule of law.[47] Admission of the civil law has been very sparing because laws can only be made and unmade by Act of Parliament. English law has admitted civil law under certain restrictions and civil law is followed in the Court of the Constable and Marshal, the Court of Admiralty and the ecclesiastical courts dealing with marriage and divorce. Hale records with approval that the clergy desired that children born before marriage should be legitimated by the subsequent marriage of the mother but the nobility rejected the proposal with reason enough on account of long usage to the contrary. Nevertheless a writ of prohibition can be issued in the common law courts if these inferior courts exceed their jurisdiction.

The Court of Admiralty claimed a jurisdiction relating to contracts or injuries incurred upon the high seas.[48] Such contracts were limited to those concerning navigation, shipping and maritime affairs and there was no jurisdiction relating to the sale of goods. Even in matters where the Court of Admiralty had jurisdiction the courts of common law had a concurrent jurisdiction. With regard to contracts relating to navigation made overseas the Court of Admiralty claimed jurisdiction, while the common law courts claimed that they had sole jurisdiction.

The treatise deals with the jurisdiction of the courts of common law in civil cases between party and party on the high seas, such cases arising on land, such cases arising overseas, marine law, a consideration of the origins of the Admiralty jurisdiction tracing its growth from the reign of Edward III to Charles I. Hale grudgingly concedes: "I am not willing to deny the antiquity of the Admirals and Admiralty Jurisdiction, these things I grant."[49] Or again: "At the time of Edward 3 the Admirals Court either had its jurisdiction original which I am not willing to assert, or uge or at least it held a mere visible and eminent growth or increase." Hale also refers to the staple jurisdiction saying: "Although staple jurisdiction was not settled by Act of Parliament yet staples were settled by patents and by consent of merchants where many things of this nature were determined."[50]

The object of the treatise was to show that although the Court of Admiralty had a limited jurisdiction and applied a procedure adopted from Roman law, the common law courts had a concurrent jurisdiction and the Court of Admiralty was accountable to the common law courts if it exceeded its jurisdiction. There was clearly a conflict between the Court of Admiralty and the courts of common law about contracts relating to navigation made overseas. The Court of Admiralty thought that it was reasonable that it should have jurisdiction over all contracts about navigation wherever made, while the courts of common law were attempting to limit the Admiralty jurisdiction to acts done on the high seas.

Hale was frequently concerned with questions of jurisdiction between courts, and in this treatise he took particular pains to establish that the common law courts had a concurrent jurisdiction. At a time when officials were paid by fees there was frequently competition between courts for business, and there is no doubt that Hale had a preference for the common law courts over those which made use of the civil law.

11. *A Tract Concerning Naturalization*

This tract is an unpublished manuscript in the British Museum,[51] and its main interest is the light which it throws on Hale's character and prejudices. He was not in favour of any general naturalization of aliens which was evidently one of the controversial topics of the day.

He starts with the proposition that any general naturalization must extend to all nations and religions and that there could be no discrimination against particular people or customs. The arguments in favour of such general naturalization were as follows:

(a) It would increase the price of land and rents.
(b) It would encourage foreign merchants to settle here and increase the wealth of the kingdom.
(c) It would bring over manufacturers and artificers.
(d) Englishmen would be initiated in manufactures unknown to them.
(e) Seamen and merchants would benefit and wealth would be increased.

Hale had no difficulty in thinking up any number of inconveniences which would arise:

(a) If the aliens brought in little wealth they would be a burden on us. If they brought in a great deal they would drive the English out of business which would cause great discontent.
(b) It was a mistake to think that the English would be instructed in their mysteries by aliens. It was true, however, that aliens might employ the English as they did at Colchester. Hale maintained that foreigners were happier in manufacturing than the English "who have mostly their curious manufactures from the Dutch and Greek". If many aliens came over they would keep trade and manufacture to themselves and trade with each other.
(c) He foresaw difficulties about the apprenticeship of foreigners. If they had to be apprenticed few foreigners would come. If not they would be outside the control of the law and might work where they pleased.
(d) Difficulties were also envisaged in connection with the privileges of the great English cities, London, York and Bristol. What would happen if aliens were not permitted to ply their trade? If they were permitted the chances were that they would under-

K

sell the English as they were good workmen. "Artificers are a numerous, indigent, querulous company of people and if opposed by aliens may be troublesome, discontented and unquiet."

(e) There should be religious toleration not only of the Christian religion but for Jews. Turks and Mohammedans. It might be argued that true religion is so reasonable and effective that heathens may be converted and that religious literature may induce other countries to tolerate the true religion in their own countries. Hale dismisses this as wishful thinking, saying that it is far more likely that we shall be corrupted by the heathen religion than the contrary.

(f) Many foreigners would entail changes in the municipal law of England. This was the experience of other nations, and he instances the changes in the laws of Britain brought in by the Danes and Saxons.

He comes to the conclusion that naturalization should be granted sparingly and not in shoals as had happened recently, and sums up his objections as follows: "Upon the whole matter it seems to me that this proposal is to be rejected as dangerous and harmful to the Kingdom, to Religion and to the interests of the English nation as utterly unlikely to produce any considerable good to the Kingdom in any way comparable to the damage and danger thereof that this excellent boundary and rampart the laws of this Kingdom have settled and at all tenaciously observed against the innundations of the foreigners."

As a workman he does not think that the English working man compares favourably with many foreigners such as the Dutch and accurately foresees the attitude of the Englishman when faced with competition from foreigners. Nevertheless, he reflects the attitude of the typical Englishman who prefers to keep foreigners out of the country and thanks God for the Straits of Dover. "England is a fair spot of ground, a rich and convenient pasture handsomely enclosed by natural inclosure against the incursions of the alien by the sea and our laws."

12. Tract Concerning the Court of Marches in Wales

This is an unpublished manuscript in the British Museum.[52] There was evidently some debate whether the jurisdiction of the Court of Marches extended to Gloucestershire, Herefordshire, Salop and Worcestershire, and Hale as a Gloucestershire man was opposed to any such jurisdiction being exercised in his own county. He asks two questions: whether by the law already established the Court of the President and Council of the Marches of Wales have any jurisdiction in these counties; and whether if by law they have no jurisdiction it would be convenient to extend their jurisdiction.

He examines the historical evidence and comes to the conclusion that the jurisdiction of the court extended to Wales only and that there was no jurisdiction in the four English counties.

He opposes the enlargement of the jurisdiction on the following grounds:

(a) No writ of error lies from the proceedings of this court and it is clearly desirable that there should be machinery for appeal to a higher court.

(b) The English courts at Westminster undoubtedly had jurisdiction in the four English counties and it was undesirable to have two competing jurisdictions.

(c) Most of the trade of Gloucester and Worcester was with London and the links with London were much stronger than with Wales.

(d) A journey to London was much easier, safer and more convenient than a journey to Ludlow.

13. *Tract on the Powers of the King*

There are two copies of this manuscript in the British Museum[53] and it is a pity that this treatise has not been published. This was a subject that Hale was particularly well qualified to discuss. His experience in Noy's chambers as a young man must have given him special opportunities of learning about the rights and duties of the king. As Chief Baron of the Exchequer and Chief Justice of the King's Bench after the Restoration he would have been consulted on many occasions by the King and his Ministers on the subject of the powers of the king.

He starts with a discussion on government in general with particular application to England, the title of the Crown of England, the capacity of the king, allegiance, the king's prerogatives and a discussion of Parliament and the council, ecclesiastical powers of the king, his temporal powers of making laws and doing justice; temporal coercion, process and execution; voluntary jurisdictions, granting dignities, jurisdictions and liberties, power to impose taxes; power of ordering commerce and trade, dealing in detail with such matters as customs, ports, coins, weights and measures, prices, tolls, fairs and markets.

14. *The Analysis of the Law*

Hale gave a great deal of thought to the problem whether the common law could be systematized, and this book was published at the same time as *The History of the Common Law* that is to say thirty-seven years after his death. There is a manuscript copy in the British Museum.[54] It was not intended for publication, but the short preface by Hale sets out his objects so clearly that it is worth summarizing. He begins on a note of despair that it is not really possible to reduce English law to any exact logical method and that he had made several attempts without success. However, he comes to three conclusions. Firstly that it is not absolutely impossible by great effort to find some reasonably satisfactory classification of the laws of England. Secondly if an attempt is made, Hale himself or other lawyers may be able to improve and modify the classification. Thirdly although those that classify and systematize any science are not usually original thinkers themselves, yet so far as the common law is concerned if it can be systematized it will help the memory and assist study.

Hale rejects the usual division into the Common Law and Statute Law and divides the law into two main divisions, namely (a) civil rights and (b) crimes and misdemeanours. *The Analysis of the Law* deals only with civil matters and is divided into fifty-four sections.

The civil part of the law concerns:

(a) Civil rights or interests.
(b) Wrongs or injuries relative to those rights.
(c) Relief or remedies applicable to these wrongs.

Civil rights are then subdivided between:

(a) Rights of persons.
(b) Rights of things.

The rights of persons concern the persons themselves or relate to their goods and estate.

Each heading is subdivided until the law on any particular subject can be inserted in the appropriate pigeonhole.

With regard to the criminal law the last sentence of the book states: "As to pleas of the Crown and matters criminal that should here ensue they are already drawn up or perfected by me in a short tract 'Of Pleas of the Crown' which I shall add to this in due course."

This was the first attempt made to bring order into the study of English law and possibly its greatest importance lies in the fact that the method adopted was followed by Blackstone who said: "Of all schemes hitherto made public for digesting the laws of England the most natural and scientific of any, as well as the most comprehensive, appears to be that of Sir Matthew Hale . . . this distribution hath been principally followed."[55]

15. *Considerations Touching the Amendment and Alteration of Laws*

This book[56] is considered in detail in the following chapter when discussing Hale's views on law reform.

16. *Concerning the Court of the King's Bench and Common Pleas*

This treatise is published by Hargrave in *Law Tracts*, vol. 1, from a manuscript lent to him by Joseph Jekyll and some of the observations are the same as in his *Considerations Touching the Amendment of Laws*. Hargrave says that the treatise was written when Hale was Chief Baron in an attempt to compose the disputes between the Courts of King's Bench and Common Pleas.[57] It was certainly written about this time as he refers to 13 Charles II in argument.

The treatise which is quite short starts with the forms of process in the King's Bench and the jurisdiction of the court; the devices practised by the Common Pleas to counter the advantages of proceeding in the King's Bench.

Hale considered that both courts should have jurisdiction in civil actions as they had in the past. He felt that it was to the benefit of the public to have a choice of forum, a subject that is often neglected by present-day reformers. It is untidy to have overlapping jurisdiction but it is often a convenience to the parties, even if it is only to avoid a bad judge.

He saw clearly that the real obstacle in the way of improving the practice of the courts was the interests of the court officials. Some improvements would require an Act of Parliament but many could be made administratively. He made five specific proposals all of a very technical nature, which are of no general interest.

17. *Preface to Rolle's Abridgment*

This *Preface* was published in 1668 while Hale was Chief Baron of the Exchequer on the authority of the Lord Keeper, Sir Orlando Bridgeman and the other judges at Westminster, namely John Kelynge, Matthew Hale, Edward Atkyns, Thomas Twisden, Christopher Turner, Wadham Wyndham, John Archer, Richard Raynford and William Morton.[58] Publication of Rolle's *Abridgment* was ordered with the direct object of educating students of the common law. We do not know whose idea it was but it is likely to have been Hale's, as he wrote the preface. The *Abridgment* is written in law French whilst the *Preface* is in English and contains 940 folio pages.

The *Preface* starts with a word of warning to the student. Rolle was an excellent man of great learning and a good judge but the *Abridgment* has many shortcomings. It was only intended for Rolle's own private use; the cases are not fully reported and much of the material is secondhand; it was never revised for publication by the author.

Hale explains that firstly the common laws of England are not the product of the wisdom of some one man or society of men in one age but the wisdom, counsel, experience and observations of many ages of wise and observing men. Experience shows that statute law cannot provide for every contingency which may arise. Secondly the common laws are settled and known. The defect of statute law is that statutes are "either too strict or too loose, too narrow or too wide" and continually require amendment. However good they are it takes time for them to get known. He maintains that an imperfect body of law known to everyone is better than a perfect new law which has to be learnt by everyone. Thirdly the common law is more detailed than other laws. This means that the laws are more numerous and less systematic than other laws and take longer to study. Nevertheless it has the advantage of being more certain and prevents arbitrariness in judges.

He has advice to give to the student on how he should set about a study of the common law. First he should spend about two or three years reading Littleton, Perkins, Doctor and Student, Fitzherbert's *Natura Brevium*, Coke's *Commentaries* and possibly his reports. He should then get a large commonplace book and divide it into alphabetical titles using Brook's *Abridgment* as a precedent. After this he should read the Year Books but as much in the Year Books is now out of date he should concentrate on the last part of Edward III the *Book of Assizes*, the second part of Henry VI, Edward IV, Henry VII, and then on to Plowden, Dyer, and Coke's *Reports* and any new reports recently printed. As he reads he should compare the cases with Rastal's *Entries* which is the best so far as the Year Books are concerned. When reading he should make an abstract of what he reads and enter it in his commonplace book in its proper place with cross-references if necessary. The student will make many mistakes, but in course of time he will become adept and what he has read will be easily available to him under the appropriate title. Constant reference to the commonplace book will also help to fix what is there in his memory and be an aid to ready reference.

Rolle's *Abridgment* is divided into general alphabetical titles containing most of the material titles of the common law and these titles are divided into general heads and these again into more particular heads. Hale indicates that the main advantage to the student in using this *Abridgment* is that he will have here abstracted in one volume all the law which is material. The *Abridgment* of Fitzherbert and Brook take the law up to the end of the reign of Henry VIII or, at the farthest, Queen Mary, while Rolle takes it to the end of Charles I and later. The Student may see in Rolle at a glance all the law relating to one subject, and the *Abridgment* will form the basis of the commonplace book.

18. *The History of the Common Law*

This book was first published anonymously in 1713 and reprinted with Hale's name attached in 1716. A third edition appeared in 1739. The fourth to sixth editions (1779–1826) were edited by Serjant Runnington with a preface containing a short life of Hale and some notes.[59] It should be noted that the book was not published until thirty-seven years after Hale's death and then not by authority.

The book is divided into twelve chapters starting with a description of *lex scripta* and the records upon which they are based. Chapters follow on *leges non scriptae,* the excellence of the common law, the original sources of English law, how the common lay stood at the time of King William I, the similarity of the laws of England and Normandy, laws made from William I to Edward II, from Edward II to his own time, the introduction of the common law into Ireland, Wales, Isle of Man, Jersey and Guernsey; its influence on the law of Scotland, the course of descent in England, trials by jury.

Maitland, as an historian and judging the book as a history of the common law, found it wanting.[60] Holdsworth on the other hand, regarded it as the ablest introductory sketch of the history of English law that appeared until Pollock and Maitland in 1895.[61] Both may be right. If the book was not intended as a history of the common law then it is not surprising that Maitland came to that conclusion.

It is tentatively suggested that the book may have been written for the benefit of law students. The last stage of a student's training was to attend the courts at Westminster Hall and the judges frequently explained points of law for the benefit of the students. The judges at that time had a teaching function which many of them took seriously. All the judges of the courts at Westminster authorized the publication of Rolle's *Abridgment* in 1668 and approved the preface written by Hale for the use of students. It is certain that Hale took the teaching function of a judge seriously as is evidenced by his preface to Rolle's *Abridgment. The History of the Common Law* may have been transcribed and circulated as notes for the use of students.

There is certain internal evidence that the book was intended for students:

(a) Choice of subject matter. Chapter XII deals with trials by jury and in Chapter VIII there is a disquisition on pleadings and reasons for increase of business in the courts since the time of Edward I, while Chapter XI deals with the law of descent in England. All these questions are vital for every practitioner and subjects which the student must learn.

(b) The style of the book is personal as if the writer is lecturing with frequent use of the personal pronouns.

(c) He sets nothing out in detail which can be found elsewhere. For example, in third edition Ch. I, p. 6, when referring to the laws of Henry I, he says: "The entire collection of these is entered in the Red Book of the Exchequer, and from thence are transcribed and published by the care of Sir Roger Twisden in the latter end of Mr Lambart's Book before mentioned." Or, on p. 5: "Mr Selden in his Book called 'Janus Anglorum' has given a full Account of these laws; so that at present it will be sufficient for me briefly to collect the Heads or Divisions of them under the reigns of these several Kings wherein they were made."

It has all the marks of an outline for students pointing out to them where they can find their authorities.

(d) Hale makes a list of all the statutes which are on the record at the time of writing, p. 17. He says that the information he gives is based on a careful enquiry made thirty years before and he does not know what have been found since. This is basic information the student must know.

(e) This book is in the nature of a commendation of common law. Chapter III p. 44 says it "is the common rule for the administration of common justices in this great Kingdom of which it has been always tender, and there is great reason for it, for it is not only a very just and excellent law in itself, but it is singularly accommodated to the frame of the English Government and to the disposition of the English nation".

(f) Finally the book was in fact used as a student's text book, which indicates that it was regarded as suitable for that purpose. Sir Thomas Reeve, Chief Justice of the Common Pleas 9 George II, in advising his nephew who was studying law, said that during the second stage of study he should read Hale's *History of the Common Law* and "Rolle's Abridgment, in the preface; in which last you will find the best scheme for studying the law now extant".[62]

19. *Tract Concerning the Law of Nature*

This tract is unpublished and there are two manuscripts in the British Museum. Harl. MS. 7159 Art. 1 states that the original in Hale's own handwriting was lent to Sir Robert Southwell by Hale's grandson Matthew and copied from the original on 19th August 1696.

Hale considers the nature of law in general and defines it as follows:

A law I take to be a rule of moral action given to a being endowed with understanding and will by him that hath power and authority to give the same and exact obedience thereunto per modum imperii commanding or forbidding such action under some penalty expressed or implicitly contained in such law. . . . (1) For the constitution of a law truly and properly so called there must be an author thereof as a legislator. (2) That the person that is lawgiver must be distinct from the person to whom it is given or that is to be obliged by it. And the reason is plain. There doth and must necessarily by every law truly so called arise an obligation from the party to whom the law is given unto the party by whom it is given to observe and perform it.

He then sets out his basic views on sovereignty that in most cases of constitutional government the sovereign is by the laws of the state and the laws of God bound by his own law because the sovereign as well as those governed is bound by the law of *'fides est servanda'*. And if the sovereign is bound by this law so also are individual men in their contracts one with the other. So long as a contract continues and is not released by the other party it stands under the law of God and to be observed by all men.

He then goes on to deal with parental powers, civil power, customary laws, punishment, different kinds of law, and finally, in Chapter IV, describes the law of nature. Man must be regarded as an intellectual and voluntary agent, and the law of nature concerns those actions controlled by the will. The laws of nature are the laws of moral righteousness discoverable by men by means of their reason and conscience. It is not easy to say what are the laws of nature, but it is best to look at the common experience of men and what are regarded as such by the common consent of civilized nations. Some of the most important natural laws are given in the Ten Commandments, while the Gospels are a full system of all excellent and moral precepts of the natural law commanding all things that are good. Hale equates the natural law with the Christian religion. A man should not injure his neighbour but may use all just means for his own preservation.

The Original Institution Power and Jurisdiction of Parliament (book of doubtful authorship)

Rigg, in the *Dictionary of National Biography*, states that in his opinion this book is undoubtedly spurious and was not written by Hale. It was published in London in 1707 and in this edition it is stated that it was a manuscript of the late Judge Hales. It is nowhere stated that it was written by him, although the manuscript was clearly in Hale's possession at the time of his death. There are two manuscript copies in the British Museum,[63] but there is no indication on these copies that they were written by Hale. The style is not Hale's and it is merely a guide-book to the practice of Parliament with all the authorities quoted. After some general sections on the persons who constitute Parliament, the duty of the Speaker, the author continues with very short chapters on specific subjects such as petitions, trial in Parliament, privileges, committees, the duty of the judges, behaviour in the House, practice relating to bills and the relationship between the two Houses. There is no reason to doubt that Rigg's opinion is correct and that the book was not written by Hale.

NOTES

1 J. B. Williams, *Life of Hale*, pp. 267–8.
2 Hale, *Summary of the Pleas of the Crown*, 1682 ed., preface, p. 4.
3 ibid., p. 5.
4 Hale, *The History of the Pleas of the Crown*, 1763, the proemonium.
5 ibid.
6 Hale, *The History of the Pleas of the Crown*, frontispiece.
7 ibid., preface p. xvi.
8 ibid.
9 ibid., p. xviii.
10 Francis Hargrave, introduction to Hale's *Jurisdiction of the Lord's House*, p. cv.
11 ibid., p. ccxv.
12 ibid., p. ccxviii.
13 ibid., p. ccxviii.
14 Hale, *Jurisdiction of Lord's House*, p. 205.
15 Holdsworth, vol. VI, p. 584.
16 "Note on Sir W. Holdsworth's article on Sir Matthew Hale and Hobbes", *Law Quarterly Review*, vol. xxxvii, p. 274.
17 ibid., p. 281.
18 Thomas Hobbes, *Elements of Law*, p. 81.
19 Add. MS. 18235 f. 2 Harl MS. 4990 Art. 3.
20 Holdsworth, vol. V, appendix III, p. 501.
21 ibid., p. 502.
22 ibid., p. 503.
23 ibid., p. 503.
24 ibid., p. 503.
25 ibid., p. 504.
26 ibid., p. 504.
27 ibid., p. 505.
28 ibid., p. 507.
29 ibid., p. 508.
30 ibid., p. 509.
31 ibid., p. 509.
32 ibid., p. 511.
33 ibid., p. 511.

34   ibid., p. 511.
35   ibid., p. 512.
36   ibid., p. 512.
37   Hale, *A Short Treatise Touching Sheriffs' Accompts*, Epistle Dedicatory, p. 3.
38   ibid., p. 49.
39   ibid., pp. 77–8.
40   ibid., p. 103.
41   ibid., p. 107.
42   ibid., p. 108.
43   ibid., p. 105.
44   Hargrave's *Tracts*, part I, preface, p. xiv.
45   Hargrave MS. 137 and Hargrave MS. 93.
46   Using Hargrave MS. 137, p. 3.
47   ibid., p. 6.
48   ibid., p. 20.
49   ibid., p. 119.
50   ibid., p. 127.
51   Stowe MS. 143 ff. 107–21b.
52   Add. MS. 41661 ff. 156–72.
53   Add. MS. 14291 ff. 212. Extract from treatise on English Government Lansdowne MS. 632. On the laws of England.
54   Harl MS. 711 Art. I.
55   Wm. Blackstone, *An Analysis of the Laws of England*, preface, p. vii.
56   Hargrave, *Tracts*, vol. I, p. 253, Add. MS. 18234.
57   Hargrave, *Tracts*, vol. I, preface, p. xiv.
58   *Collectanea Juridica*, vol. I, no. ix, pp. 266–7.
59   Holdsworth, vol. VI, p. 585.
60   Maitland, "Material for English Legal History", *Collected Works*, vol. II, no. 5.
61   Holdsworth, vol. VI, p. 586.
62   Lord Chief Justice Reeve's instructions to his nephew concerning the study of the law, *Collectanea Juridica*, vol. I, E. and R. Brooke, London, 1791, p. 79.
63   On Parliament. Add. MS. 33249 f. 1 and Treatise on Parliament attributed to late seventeenth century Add. MS. 36858.

XV

Law Reform

Hale's views on law reform are contained in a manuscript entitled *Considerations Touching Amendment or Alterations of Laws* which can be found in Hargrave's *Tracts*, vol. I. The first sentence sets the tone of the whole manuscript. "The business of amendment or alteration of laws is a choice and tender business neither wholly to be omitted when the necessity requires, and yet very cautiously and warily to be undertaken, though the necessity may, or at least may seem to require it."[1] He then considers the two extremes:

1. The error in the excess, the over busy and hasty and violent attempt in mutation of laws under pretence of reformation.
2. The error in the defect, a wilful and over strict adhering in every particular to the continuance of the laws in the state we find them, though the reformation of them be never so necessary, safe and easy.[2]

Touching the first error he states that the old law has an advantage over any new law in that it is better known to the people who are concerned with it, and that before any change is made it must be shown that there is a substantial advantage in the new law over the old.

In his view it was only through time and long experience that it could be known what was workable or not, and the acutest intellects could not foresee all the variety of circumstances which might and do arise in practice.

Now a law that hath abidden the test of time, hath met with most of these varieties and complications. . . . So that in truth ancient laws, especially those that have a common concern, are not the issues of the prudence of this or that council or statute, but are the production of the various experiences and applications of the wisest thing in the inferior world; to wit time which as it discovers day after day new inconveniences, so it doth successively apply new remedies; and indeed it is a kind of aggregation of the discoveries, results and applications of ages and events; so that it is a great adventure to go about to alter it without very grave necessity, and under the greatest demonstration of safety and convenience imaginable.[3]

He adds other reasons that too many amendments lead to uncertainty, that people don't like it. He says that when William I arrived in England he introduced many Norman customs and laws, but when things began to settle he found it not only convenient but necessary to restore the old laws "especially those that obtained upon the account and reverence of Edward the Confessor".

He then goes on to lay down three principles always to be borne in mind when considering changes in the law:

1. That the change be demonstrably for the better, and such as cannot introduce any considerable inconvenience in the other end of the wallet.
2. That the change, though most clearly for the better, be not in foundations or principles, but in such things as may be consistent with the general frame and basis of government or law.
3. That the changes be gradual, and not too much at once, or at least more than the exigency of things required.[4]

He then considers why some men have this passion for changing the law.

1. Man is by nature fond of change and some men pine for it even in those cases where change is hurtful, such as the form of government or law. The very same itch of novelty and innovation, that carries some dispositions to novelty in garbs and gestures, or to new fashions in clothes, carries such when they happen to be in place to innovations and new fashions in law; a certain restlessness and nauseousness in what they have, and a giddy humour after something which is new, or possibly upon some over expectation of the benefit of such change, though they have no full nor perfect notion of what is to be introduced in the place of what they nauseate.[5]
2. A man may have personally suffered under the existing laws and so want a change. "For there is in mankind a passionate self-law, which makes men think that whatsoever crosseth them in their interest or concern is unjust, and fit to be altered."[6]
3. By reason of a failure to understand the true nature of law and government the false hope that the perfect law might be made. "And hence if there once occur any inconvenience in a law, presently away with it, and a new frame or model must be excogitated and introduced, and then all will be well. But this is a great error; for it is most certain, that when all the wisdom and prudence, and forecast in the world is used, all human things will still be imperfect. . . . And the reason is apparent; because

it concerns the manners of many men, which are so various, uncertain and complicated, both in themselves and the circumstances adhering to them, that they are not possibly to be exactly fitted." He shows that when a new situation arises the law may be amended without a total alteration of the law so that the alteration does not constitute a new law, but amends the old one "so that it still morally continues the same law".[7]

4. Many men suggest alterations in laws when they are ignorant of the laws it is proposed to change. Men are often provoked and irritated by things which they do not know and understand and this is particularly so of the highly intelligent or intellectual, or those who think themselves so, and are impatient of what they do not know. "They think the laws are foolish; because if they were reasonable things, they must understand them without study, as they do the force of an argument. . . . They that are but half sighted in the business of the law, are more ready with speed and peremptoriness to pronounce for its alteration, than they that look about them and see this whole business before them."[8]

5. Men whose attention is fixed upon a certain specific reform do not always appreciate the inconvenience which it may bring in its wake. "But the great business of a reformer is not only to see that his remedy is apposite, but that it does not introduce some other considerable inconvenience."[9]

6. Certain passions spur men on to amend the law; vain glory, ambition, fear (on the part of a ruler), envy and malice at the legal profession.

Hale then considers the stubborn resistance to any change in law which is encountered.

1. By long use and custom, men, especially old men and lawyers, contract a superstitious veneration beyond what is just and reasonable. They tenaciously retain the forms and practices which though at first useful and reasonable have become burdensome and inconvenient.

2. An over-jealous fear that it may be possible that some unthought of inconvenience may emerge which may introduce some unexpected mischief to the community.

3. The fear of offending great officers and ministers of justice. Hale saw clearly that one of the great difficulties of reform was the system whereby officials had paid for their appointments and there was a vested interest in carrying on the system in the same way and any reform which might cut down their perquisites would be strongly resisted.

4. A fear that a small reform may be the thin edge of the wedge and that a major attack may be made on the existing system.

5. Attempts at law reform having been so unsuccessful of recent times, "the very name of reformation and a reformer begins to

be a style or name of contempt or obloquy; for men are as fearful to be under the imputation of a reformer of the law, as they would be of the name of knave or fool or hypocrite".[10]

But despite all the difficulties he thinks "that good and wise men may and ought to make some prudent essay even in this great business" and he puts forward certain propositions.

1. There are good examples in history particularly the reform of Roman law undertaken by Justinian. The work was undertaken by twenty lawyers under Trebonianus and completed in three years although there were over 2,000 volumes of law to digest. He then refers to the reforms of Edward I in England, reforming the whole system in Wales. He fixed the jurisdiction of the Higher Courts to 40s. and upwards, prohibited the alienation of land in mortmain, made the county liable to answer for robberies in its jurisdiction, prohibited the creation of new tenures, limited the jurisdiction of the ecclesiastical courts. He states that for the last forty years little has been done because the times had been tumultuous and not seasonable and consequently there is more need for it now.

2. That the law is a human institution so that abuses creep in and like ivy on a tree will strangle it in time. But if these abuses are investigated it is found that they are often concerned with the profit to be made out of the law. It is the abuses which require attention and not the law itself.

3. There are however some parts of the law itself which require amendment as well as the abuses. "And we must remember that laws were not made for their own sakes, but for the sake of those who were to be guided by them."[11] If they do not fulfil this purpose they must be amended or new laws made. They do not fulfil their purpose when they are basically wrong and unjust or become obsolete in the course of time. "He that thinks a state can be steered by the same laws in every kind, as it was two or three hundred years since, may as well imagine that clothes that fitted him when he was a child should serve him when he is a grown man. . . . All that I contend for is not to render laws of men like laws of nature fixed and unalterable, but that it [reform] be done with great prudence, advice, care, and upon a clear prospect of the whole business."[12]

4. During the course of time the number of laws becomes excessive unless they are pruned and reduced to a manageable size. "And the reason is, because this age for the purpose received from the last a body of laws, and they add more and transmit the whole to the next age, and they add to what they had received and transmit the whole stock to the next age. Then as the rolling of a snowball it increases in bulk in every age, till it becomes utterly unmanageable."[13]

5. There are in the law some things although possibly of ordinary

use and occurrences which would not be missed if they were cut out.

6. "The amendment of things amiss timely by knowing able and judicious men that understand their business, may do very much good, and prevent very much evil that may otherwise ensue."[14] He fears however that in his day this usually happens too late and that judges and lawyers will do nothing to the law and therefore it falls into other hands.

Hale then considers the manner, the persons and the timing of law reform. With regard to the manner and persons he makes certain observations:

1. That it be done deliberately and leisurely.
2. That every point be fully debated and impartially examined.
3. That wherever possible it should be done by the courts and not by the legislature. Unnecessary applications to Parliament sometimes breed unexpected inconveniences.
4. Where the legislature intervenes let it be precise and particular.
5. There should be no retrospective legislation "but let the time that they shall be put into execution have such a prospect as men may not be surprised by the change of things, but may be fitted and prepared for it".[15]
6. The preparation of bills should only be undertaken upon the express authority of the king with the advice of both Houses of Parliament by "the judges or other sages of the law" and he would have no busybody intermeddle who was not instructed by the executive. Such bills should be presented to the House of Commons in the first place and when read for the second time the judges should be called in to the debate at the committee of the House.

With regard to the timing of measures of law reform he observes that it is not every Parliament that is fit for such business. They should not be brought in when times are turbulent and busy but when there is peace at home and little trouble abroad. He observes that when Cromwell was in power there was a great desire for law reform but those that were asked to undertake the business would not do so. Hale says that many of the reforms desired were good, but men felt that Cromwell's rule would not last and the king would return again and it would be better not to upset the existing law in the meantime. "The things desired were many of them for the matter good; but the end and design and the state and conditions of things would not allow of such an undertaking."[16]

After these general remarks on law reform Hale then deals in some detail with the specific reforms which he considers are required in his own time.

He considers some inconveniences in the management of the

king's revenue and how to rectify them. The king had a multitude of small rents some arising out of towns and others out of specific pieces of land which were expensive to collect and caused ill feeling. Hale suggests that they should all be sold and the proceeds of sale invested in land which should be let on seven-year leases at a proper economic rent. He suggests cutting down the staff who collect the king's revenue by 50 per cent. He advocates the abolition of unnecessary officers and improvements in the methods of keeping accounts. He complains of the great men who hold certain offices such as the King's Remembrancer but all the work is done by deputies. "If these officers are not necessary, why are they continued? If they are, why should they not be executed at the charge only which accrues from the deputy, and the benefit of the nominal officer that doth nothing be retrenched as a needless charge?"[17] He thinks that the officers should only be paid for what they do and that they should be educated and experienced men and not courtiers or great men. He adds that there should be no sale of these offices, and that it would pay the king to award pensions to those who have served him rather than give them an office as a perquisite. His proposed remedy is an Act of Parliament abolishing the offices and compensating those removed by a pension.

Reforms relating to the Courts of Justice and the County Court are then considered. Actions where the debt or damage did not exceed 40s. had to be heard by the County Courts and not by the courts in Westminster. This was established by Edward I and in his day 40s. was a considerable sum. By Hale's time this sum was worth only 5s. and he says that money was much dearer in the time of Edward I than in his day as there was more of it in later times. Prices were higher than they used to be. He gives examples of the prices in Edward I's time: fat ox 24s., fat cow 12s., a fat hog 40d., a fat mutton unshorn 20d., a fat hen 1d. and twenty-four eggs 1d.

He agrees that it was a wise provision to keep small suits away from the courts in Westminster but that the monetary limit should be increased to £10 to cover the effects of inflation. He argues that the costs of coming to Westminster are disproportionate to the amount claimed. The number of actions at Westminster has increased, the costs have increased, and the attorneys and solicitors have increased. There had been several attempts to deal with the problem by statute in the time of Elizabeth I and James I but they had proved ineffectual because of the vested interests of the legal profession and court officials and the decay of the County Courts. The choice at the time was between expensive justice at Westminster or little or none in the County Courts.

L

He suggests that County Courts should be re-established locally. This suggestion was in fact not carried into effect by Parliament until 1846. Each court should have a judge or steward being a barrister of not less than seven years standing who should be paid a salary out of the county rates; the steward should try causes in the presence of a jury of twelve; the perquisites of the court should be paid to the king; there should be a clerk to keep the records; the number of attornies permitted to practise should be limited to six in each county, appointed and removed by the Chief Justice of the Common Pleas; jurisdiction should be limited to debt or damage up to £5; the process should be only by summons, attachment, and distress and executed only by means of fieri facias, i.e. execution on goods and chattels. It follows from these proposals that the courts at Westminster should not entertain actions for debt or damages under £5 unless the title to land was at issue, and if a plaintiff insisted on proceeding at Westminster he would recover no costs above the amount of the debt or damages.

He explains that his proposals are merely an extension of the old jurisdiction established by Edward I. In his view a professional lawyer is more fitted to act as judge than a few ignorant and perhaps interested suitors, trial by jury is better than wagers of law, and £5 is not even as much as 40s. at the time of Edward I.

He argues that these proposals would be of great convenience to people, the courts at Westminster would be freed from a number of petty suits, and it would prevent a number of oppressive suits where men were sued for a trifle so that if successful the plaintiff could recover costs often forty times more than the amount of the debt, which might be crushing to the defendant.

One interesting side effect suggested by Hale is "that students and professors of law, which are now generally driven or drawn to London, so that there are scarce any left in the country, will have some encouragement to reside in the country, and the country will not be left to the management of attornies and solicitors".[18]

The Court of Common Pleas, which he calls "the great orb, wherein the greater business between party and party doth or should move"[19] is the next court to receive Hale's attention. His first observation is that there are too many officials and too many separate offices often at different places to deal with each step in an action. He proposes that there should be one office only under one officer who would have clerks and officers to carry out the particular steps within the office. He compares the system unfavourably with the Court of King's Bench, where the civil business is all under one official. He complains secondly about the great number of attornies all competing for business. This leads to real grievances as there is not enough business for all and attornies "shark upon the few clients they have, and are apt to use tricks and knavery to gain themselves credit with those that employ them". The attornies have so little business in court that they employ as agents other attornies who know little about it and many mistakes occur. The judges spend a good deal of their time putting right procedural mistakes, and punishing those who have caused them by their ignorance or trickery. Hale's remedy is to cut down the numbers of attornies, and he felt that this could be done without any Act of Parliament or public discussion. Many were dishonest and many incompetent and these should be weeded out. "A strict and impartial examination of this kind would cut off abundance of rubbish."[20] He appreciated that these proposals would meet a great deal of opposition from the vested interest of officials, attornies and others who benefited from the system, and in fact these interests prevailed and no such reforms were made.

About the procedure he comments on the unnecessary fees, the fact that trials did not go on from day to day but were adjourned to another fixed date, and also that the right of audience was limited to serjeants-at-law. Serjeants were men learned in the law and usually appointed late in life who continued until an advanced age. He recommended that all members of the bar should have a right of audience so that the litigant could choose a counsel most fitted to conduct his business and not be limited to those barristers who were also serjeants. He thought that it was valuable that both the Court of Common Pleas and Court of King's Bench should have jurisdiction in civil actions and that a plaintiff should have the choice in which court he should take his proceedings.

The Court of Common Pleas was strangled by all these offices of profit and unnecessary practices and suitors found that the business could be dealt with more expeditiously in the Court of King's Bench. It is one of the facts of litigation that business flows to the court where there is a good judge and the road to the judge is unimpeded by unnecessary technicalities.

At the beginning of Chapter V of Hargrave's *Tracts* Hale sets out the particular matters that needed reform and apart from those already mentioned he proposed to deal with the inconveniences relating to the passing and charging of estates in land; the inconveniences in pleas of the Crown; and the inconveniences in the present collection of statutes and books of the law. Unfortunately there is no trace of his comments on the reform of the land law and criminal law, but his recommendations on the books of the law are in manuscript. In the British Museum bound in one volume[21] is the manuscript from which Hargrave published his tract and also an earlier manuscript which covers books of the law.

Hale considers that the king should appoint some lawyers to collect together all the statutes which are in use or in force and reduce them to one short volume under alphabetical titles. He appreciates that there would also have to be certain revisions and that this could not be done without the authority of Parliament. This volume should be examined and authorised by Parliament as the volume of statutes. Examples of the titles given by him are clergy, alehouses, recusants, bankrupts and forcible entries, and Hale says: "It would appear a work becoming the care of a Prince to make or order such a reduction. This was attempted by the command of King James by many learned persons and brought into a fair progress. But it died."

What is said about the statutes can also be said about the books of the common law, and Hale mentioned that these books had increased enormously in the last fifty years, not only reports but tracts, many of them being contradictory. Many of the reports contained law which was out of date, and he estimated that it would take a man nine or ten years to read all the published books on law.

He says: "I would advise one large and authentical abridgment of the Books and Tracts of the law reduced under apt and alphabetical titles as has been attempted by Brooke and Fitzherbert. Brooke is too curt and concise; Fitzherbert is large enough but the titles are too general. Both are defective in that they do not take in the law after Queen Elizabeth which is more voluminous than what went before." The abridgment should cut out all titles which are out of date or contrary to current practice or altered by subsequent Acts of Parliament. "This would pare off from this abridgment a great deal of impertinence and unnecessary furniture which though possibly it may be useful for curiosity or antiquity as are the books of Glanvill, Fleta, Bracton, Britton, Thornton yet they are but stuffing and not useful for a Digest of the Law."

In such an abridgment doubtful points of law could be settled and he gives examples of things which should be left out of the abridgment. He suggests that writs of right could be left out as he only remembered one or two cases in forty years' experience and these had come to nothing because of procedural difficulties. He adds that "an attempt of this nature is only possible to be effected by the joint undertaking and assistance of learned and judicious men, but would be a foundation of much honour to the Kingdom and of peace and settlement of questions of law".

Hale considered carefully the subject of the enrollment of deeds

as a form of land registration. Somers includes in his collection of
tracts "Lord Chief Justice Hale's Treatise showing how useful,
safe, reasonable and beneficial the enrolling and registering of all
conveyances of lands may be to the inhabitants of this Kingdom"
(Somers *Tracts*, vol. IV, p. 81). This treatise is only ascribed to
Hale but from internal evidence and the style it is fairly certain
that it was written by him. There is also a manuscript in the British
Museum on the same subject dated 1668.[22]

In his usual orderly way he discusses the mischief to be remedied
and the remedy to be applied. There is no doubt about the mischief
as purchasers are often deceived and creditors defeated, and there
were many law suits resulting from secret charges or mortgages
on property not disclosed. The remedy proposed was a deeds registry to enrol or register all conveyances and documents of title. This
was a method subsequently used in Yorkshire and Middlesex before it was superseded by the registration of land at a central land
registry. Hale argued that if the inconveniences introduced by the
scheme were greater than the benefits it should be rejected. To be
of value there must be no loopholes and the registry must cover
all documents of title. "For if one leak be unstopped, the vessel will
sink as if more were open." He then considers whether this scheme
is a practical proposition in the circumstances of his times. "Indeed it is a fine thing in the theory and speculation, and a man
that fixeth his thoughts upon the good that might come by such
an expedient, without troubling himself with the difficulties that lie
in the way to it, may drive it on very earnestly; but he that shall
consider the difficulty of it, will easily see that it is but a notion
and speculation and cannot be effected or reduced into practice, at
least not without immense confusion." Hale concludes that it
would be necessary to produce authentic deeds for registration, but
this raises the question of those who have possession without any
deed, or cannot bring the deed as it is in the possession of some
other person, or have lost their deeds in the Civil War. He asks
whether intermediate deeds on the title should be enrolled and if
so he thinks the sheer physical problem of registration would be
enormous and estimates in London alone 40,000 deeds would have
to be enrolled, which could only be contained in 230 volumes of
vellum books.

He appreciates all the difficulties and asks where the registry is
to be, if in London people would have to come to London to register their deeds, which would be intolerable. If in the country
where the land lies vendors and purchasers of country estates
dealing in London would be forced to search the register in Corn-
wall or Northumberland where the land might be.

After weighing up all the advantages and disadvantages he comes to the conclusion that the disadvantages outweigh the advantages. "Upon the whole matter, I think that the compulsion of every man to enroll or register his writings and evidences of his land, whether past of future, under any penalty, is impractical, and utterly inconvenient and dangerous to men's estates." He considers that it is a system which can be successfully applied in small areas but not in a great kingdom. This is the method adopted in the twentieth century to bring in compulsory registration of land. Starting in London it spread to Middlesex and adjacent counties and in process of time should cover the whole of England.

Hale thought that codification of the law was possible and desirable. In the preface to *The Analysis of the Law* he admits that the law is so various "that I cannot reduce it to an exact logical method . . . but it is not altogether impossible by much attention and labour to reduce the laws of England at least into a tolerable method or distribution". He thought that by making his *Analysis* he would give the opportunity for himself and others to make suggestions for reform which might occur to him during the course of writing and in this way pave the way for a better and more methodical system of law. During a discussion with friends on whether or not it was possible to systematize the common law Hale took some paper and wrote out some headings showing how it could be done. His friends pressed him to make the attempt himself but he replied that it was not the work for one man but should only be undertaken by order of the State together with other men learned in the law. In his *Preface to Rolle's Abridgment* he says that law does go out of date and it is to be wished that there should be a *corpus juris,* but this is a work of time and requires many industrious and judicious hands to assist in it. He thus anticipates the setting up by Act of Parliament in 1964 of the Law Commission composed of men of learning and experience under the chairmanship of a judge empowered to codify, prune and keep the law continuously under review and up to date.

NOTES

1 *Considerations touching the Amendment or Alteration of Laws,* Hargrave's *Tracts,* vol. I, p. 253; taken from Add. MS. 18234 in British Museum dated August 1665.
2 ibid., p. 253.
3 ibid., p. 254.
4 ibid., p. 256.
5 ibid., pp. 256–7.

6   ibid., p. 257.
7   ibid., p. 257.
8   ibid., pp. 261–2.
9   ibid., p. 262.
10 ibid., p. 266.
11 ibid., p. 269.
12 ibid., p. 269.
13 ibid., p. 270.
14 ibid., p. 271.
15 ibid., p. 273.
16 ibid., p. 274.
17 ibid., p. 279.
18 ibid., p. 284.
19 ibid., p. 284.
20 ibid., p. 286.
21 Add. MS. 18234.
22 Add. MS. 41661 ff. 227–35b.

XVI

Legal Influence

Hale is commonly regarded as an historian as well as a lawyer but it must be doubted whether he was an historian in the modern sense of the word. F. W. Maitland was a true historian, and it is said of him that he tried to divest himself of all prejudices and preconceptions and lose himself in the documents of the period that he was studying that he would be able to think the thoughts of mediaeval man after them.[1] To Maitland "Legal documents, documents of the most technical kind are the best, often the only evidence that we have for social and economic history, for the history of morality, for the history of practical religion."[2] Hale was not an historian in the sense that he had a great desire to put himself in the shoes of men of an earlier time or to study social and economic history.

Hale's study of history was made as a lawyer to find out what the law was on a particular subject. He was an extremely thorough and conscientious lawyer and in the seventeenth century it was necessary to discover the law from early records. Reporting of cases was bad before the advent of shorthand and it was not safe to rely on second-hand evidence. He was a true scholar, and the principles of scholarship are the same whether used by an historian or a lawyer. He sought the truth, trying to find out what the law really was and this involved going back to original sources. Today when most of the law has been reduced to statute law and general principles it is possible for a man to be a first-class lawyer without much knowledge of legal history, but this was not the case in the seventeenth century when the common law had a much greater importance.

Burent says that Hale studied the original records in the Tower of London and certainly during the Commonwealth he intervened to save the records in the Tower from destruction. In his library he had made a great collection of transcripts of petitions in Parliament, Close Rolls and other early records and these documents form the bulk of the manuscripts which he bequeathed to Lincoln's Inn. They are in fact his tools of trade as a lawyer and the manuscripts left to Lincoln's Inn were those which he valued most highly. There is a great deal of evidence in his writings to show that he inspected the original documents. One instance will suffice. In his *History of the Common Law*,[3] when discussing Magna Carta and the Charter de Forestea, he says: "You may see transcripts of both charters verbatim in Matthew Paris and in the Red Book of the Exchequer. There were seven pairs of these charters sent to some of the Great Monasteries under the Seal of King John. One part thereof sent to the Abbey of Tewkesbury I have seen under the Seal of that King. The substance thereof differs something from the Magna Carta and Carta de Forestea granted by King Henry 3 but not very much as may appear by comparing them."

Maitland, discussing the different attitudes of the lawyer and the historian, said: "What the lawyer wants is authority and the newer the better; what the historian wants is evidence and the older the better."[4] This may be true today, when a report can be relied on for its accuracy, but in Hale's day it was the original document establishing the law which was of the greatest value. Having discovered his true authority a lawyer is content, whilst an historian will wish to draw conclusions from the facts he has discovered. Nevertheless Hale acquired a very extensive knowledge of history obtained through his study of the law and when he refers to historical facts he is likely to be accurate.

As an author a good deal of his writing on law consisted of his notebooks made for his own use as a practitioner. The voluminous *Black Book of the New Law* and his notes on Fitzherbert's *New Natura Brevium* and his notes on Coke's *First Institute* certainly come within this description, and his *History of the Pleas of the Crown* was built up on the basis of his *Summary of the Pleas of the Crown*, which was in fact a notebook.

Most of his writing on public law consists of arguments dealing with specific controversies of the day. His reply to Hobbes, the *Jurisdiction of the Lord's House*, his tract on naturalization, *A Short Treatise touching Sheriffs' Accompts* are all in effect judgments given after reviewing all the evidence which is usually of a historical nature. These are all weighty judgments which rest on great historical knowledge and learning. The other manuscripts on public law relate in some way to the rights of the king such as the treatise in three parts on the customs and the manuscript on the powers of the king.

Hale never sat down to write a book on a legal subject for publication. He took naturally to writing to set down his thoughts and clear his mind. His objects in writing were limited. He advised students to keep a common place book and build up an abridgment of their own as it was a method of ready reference and helped the memory. This was how the *Black Book of the New Law* grew up. When a careful examination of historical events has to be made to trace the source of an institution such as in the *Jurisdiction of the Lord's House* it is essential to commit the sequence to writing, and this he did. In other cases such as *A Treatise touching Sheriffs' Accompts* the Lord High Treasurer had asked for a report on the quarrel between the Clerks of the Pipe and the Auditors of the Exchequer, and this report would naturally be made in writing.

His *Preface to Rolle's Abridgment* was written for students and specifically addressed to them. This is evidence that he took seriously the duty of a judge to supervize and control legal education. It was the custom at that time and well on into the eighteenth century for law students to attend the courts at Westminster, and frequently judges would explain points of law for the benefit of the students. *The History of the Common Law* may or may not have been written for their benefit but it was certainly used for the purpose of legal education for a considerable time.

It is as a law reformer that Hale's views have such a modern ring. There was a hot zeal for law reform during the Commonwealth and Hale co-operated and worked hard on bills of reform. Few of these bills became law, but an Act establishing civil marriage reached the Statute Book. His general views on law reform cannot be bettered. Law reform had become associated with the Commonwealth and consequently not a matter which was suitable for discussion by the king's men. He felt however that the time was ripe for measures of law reform now that the King was back on the throne.

Hale saw clearly that some attempt at the systematization of the law would have to be made. He considered it possible but very difficult and made an initial attempt himself in his *Analysis of the Law*. He thought that this could not be done by one man but would have to be the work of a number of learned men appointed by the Government for this purpose, thus anticipating the setting up of the Law Commission in 1964. This *Analysis of the Law* is not important in itself, but it's importance lies in the fact that it was the basis upon which Blackstone built when writing his *Commentaries on the Laws of England*.

Not only did the law require systematization but it required pruning as old laws go out of date but still remain on the Statute Book or still form part of the common law. If the law is not pruned it becomes out of hand and unmanageable. If law becomes uncertain because of a multiplicity of overlapping laws this causes unnecessary litigation and consequent expense. He thought that this pruning should be done by knowing and judicious men who understand their business at the right time and if judges and lawyers would do nothing the business of law reform might get in the hands of the wrong people. He visualized an official abridgment being made comprizing only the up-to-date law, but this would mean that Parliament would have to pass amending legislation. Three hundred years later Parliament has appointed the Law Commission not only to codify but to do the pruning which is required.

He considered that reforms should be instigated by the courts and the judges rather than by Parliament whenever this was possible and this is an aspect of law reform that has been given little consideration. He lays down the principle that Parliament should never be approached if the matter can be dealt with by the power of the court as statutes often breed unexpected inconveniences. Clearly all procedural matters are within the sphere of the courts, but often judges are disinterested or too busy to occupy themselves with this side of their work.

Hale's influence as a judge can be conveniently considered under three main headings, his personal qualities, his professional qualifications and his judicial attitudes.

1. *Personal qualities*

His most outstanding characteristic as a judge was his patience and thoroughness. He applied all his mind to the case he was trying, putting all other matters aside and concentrating on the problems before him. He ate sparingly at midday so that he would be fit for work in the afternoon and spent endless pains and time in reaching his decision, thinking it better to lose time than make a wrong judgment. He was patient with the accused and witnesses, and did not hector them in the manner which was common at the time. Judges spent a great deal more time questioning witnesses than is customary today and Hale's treatment of witnesses set a very high standard.

Hale was completely disinterested. He was not swayed by opportunities of power or money and could not be bribed. He was indifferent to the views of Oliver Cromwell and Charles II and refused to sit at the trial of Penruddock or to try honest Dissenters. He took seriously the admonition in the Prayer Book "that they indifferently minister justice to the punishment of wickedness and vice". He was equally indifferent to the solicitations of great men, and when a Duke called upon him to discuss his case before the hearing he refused to hear him. He was extremely scrupulous in money matters, refusing anything which might give an appearance of a bribe and even paying more for an article than it was worth so that men could not say that the judge was under an obligation to the vendor. He regarded it as unworthy in a judge to prefer his own interest or profit or the interests of the courts or its officers above the public interest, and it is for this reason that his views on the reform of the law courts are of particular value.

He had great intellectual honesty and although he resisted pressure from the Government to try Penruddock and the Dissenters if he had in fact sat as a judge and found them guilty at law he would not have refused to convict. He had sworn to do justice in accordance with the law and this he would do at all costs, however distasteful it might be to him personally or to his ideas of justice. A very good example of this is the case of Robert Atkins *v.* Holford Clare, Ventris I, p. 399. The plaintiff was seized of seven hundreds in Gloucestershire and the defendant, the sheriff, executed several writs in these hundreds. The plaintiff claimed that liberties had been granted to these hundreds in days gone by and that writs could only be executed there through the bailiff of the liberty. Hale in his judgment surveyed the historical evidence in favour of the plaintiff and came to the reluctant conclusion that he was right. He said, "I would have given judgment another way both for the general concern and for the sake of the County of Gloucester which I know will suffer much by this thing." Nevertheless he was constrained to give judgment for the plaintiff as he had a right at law, however objectionable and outdated it might be. He suggested that there should be a short Act of Parliament of three lines to put it right and abolish these liberties. In fact he said he had once drafted such a bill and wished someone would now promote it in Parliament.

Although so eminent in his profession he did not value himself too highly and was willing to listen to others. When giving judgment he always encouraged counsel to interrupt if he had made a mistake so that it could be put right immediately.

2 Professional Qualifications

Hale was a lawyer of long and varied practical experience. His younger days were spent in Noy's chambers when he had a great deal of conveyancing experience and also acquired special knowledge of the affairs of the King. He was a judge of the Court of Common Pleas under Cromwell, Chief Baron of the Court of Exchequer and Chief Justice of the Court of King's Bench under

Charles II, being on the Bench for over twenty years and serving
in all the common law courts.

Burnet reports Hale as saying, "A little law, a good tongue, and
a good memory, would fit a man for the Chancery; and he said it
was a golden practice, for the lawyers there got more money than
in all the other courts in Westminster Hall."[5] Undoubtedly when
at the Bar Hale frequently appeared in the Court of Chancery and
he spoke from personal experience.

Hale was a man of prodigious learning, rivalling Selden himself,
but his learning was mainly confined to the law. His interests were
very wide but his learning was legal. This can be demonstrated by
an examination of his most valuable manuscripts given to Lincoln's
Inn. Apart from two bibles of the fourteenth and fifteenth centuries, notes on chronology, some antiquarian papers acquired as
executor of Selden, three books on mathematics and an alchemical
treatise, all the manuscripts relate in some way to the law. A man
may be a good judge without great learning, but depth of learning
is more than an adornment to a judge. It enables him to do justice
when all the law has not been cited to him by counsel which may
be due to inadvertence or lack of knowledge and experience.

3. Judicial Attitudes

Hale was on the Bench for twenty years, but it cannot be claimed
that his judgments produced any development in the law. He was
essentially a very conservative lawyer and would not have approved
of judge-made law. Lord Mansfield in the eighteenth century was
on the Bench for thirty-two years and adapted the common law
to the needs of his day. Hale was not an innovator in this way
and would not have made such changes however long he had
been a judge. There are very few of his judgments reported
at length and, such as there are, are reported in the State Trials
series, and also in Raymond, pp. 209–39; Levinz, pt. 2, pp. 1–16;
Ventris, 1, pp. 399–429; Keble, ii, pp. 749 to end; Keble, iii,
pp. 1–622.

Hale approved of the common law because of its very particu-
larity as a prevention against arbitrariness by a judge. The common law was diffuse and difficult to learn but it dealt with a large
number of individual situations and the chances were that a party
could bring his action in the right category. "Yet certain it is that
the law is best framed that at once hath certainty and yet in-
duceth as few particular mischiefs as may be."[6] He was reluctant
as a judge to make any innovations as he said, "The expounders
must look further than the present instance, and whether such an
exposition may not introduce a greater inconvenience than its

remedies."[7] Again, "The common laws of England are more particular than other laws; and this though it renders them more numerous, less methodical, and takes up longer time for their study, yet it recompenseth with greater advantages; namely it prevents arbitrariness by the judge, and makes the law more certain, and better applicable to the business that comes to be judged by it. General laws are indeed very comprehensive, soon learned, and easily digested into method; but when they come to particular application, they are of little service, and leave a great latitude to partiality, interest, and variety of apprehensions, to misapply them."[8]

This concern about the arbitrariness of the judge frequently appears in Hale's writing. When discussing judicial decisions he says that although the decisions of the judges binds the parties to the dispute yet they do not make law properly so called for only the king and Parliament can do this. He affirms that judicial decisions have great weight and authority in expounding, declaring and publishing what the law is, especially when they follow the decisions of earlier judges. He describes judicial decisions as less than law, but they are greater evidence of what the law is than the opinion of any private person. They are so because judges are men chosen by the king as being of greater learning, knowledge and experience of the law than others; because they are on their oath to judge according to law; because they have the best assistance in arriving at a correct judgment; because their judgments are upheld until they are reversed by a higher court or set aside by statute.[9]

He distinguishes three kinds of judicial decisions: [10]

1. When law is certain but only the facts at issue, e.g. who shall succeed as heir, how much shall the wife have for her dower.
2. When the judge has to make certain deductions from the known and established law.
3. When the judge has no guide but "the common reason of the thing", e.g. construction of wills and deeds. He believed that a judge decided better than "any grave grammarian or logician or other prudent man would do and that a good common lawyer was best able to construe the intention of the testator or donor as he would have the knowledge of what judges had done in previous cases of a similar nature".[11]

Hale was equally certain that equity had nothing arbitrary about it, and Burnet quotes Serjeant Runnington as saying, "He [Hale] held equity to be not only part of the common law, but also one of its principal grounds; for which reason he reduced it to principles, that it might be studied as a science."[12]

There are always these two points of view amongst lawyers, those who seek certainty and those who look to judges to make and adapt the law. The views of Lord Radcliffe on the subject are of interest. "The truth is, in my belief, that the image of the judge, objective, impartial, erudite and experienced declarer of the law that is, lies deeper in the consciousness of civilisation than the image of the law maker, propounding what are avowedly new rules of human conduct."[13] No doubt judges do in fact innovate and adapt and amend the law but in Lord Radcliffe's view they would serve the public interest better by keeping quiet about their legislative function.

Hale considered that the common law was particularly suited to the English temperament and that the laws of one nation could not be transplanted to another as they reflected certain national characteristics. In Scotland for instance there is a greater devotion to general principles, while an Englishman is only concerned with what works in practice. Hale said: "It [the common law] is not only a very just and excellent law, but it is singularly accommodated to the frame of the English Government, and to the disposition of the English nation, and such as by a long experience and use is as it were incorporated into their very temperament, and, in a manner, become the complexion and constitution of the English Commonwealth."[14] Again he states: "And although the specific nature of Jews and Gentiles and all nations be the same, yet it is certain that there ever were and ever will be, great variety in the state disposition and concern of several people; so that that law, which would be a most wise, apt and suitable constitution to one people, would be utterly improper and inconvenient to another."[15]

Although Hale believed that new law could only be made by statute he had a great distrust for wholesale codification. In his view Parliament should intervene to correct known abuses, cut out law which had fallen into disuse and adapt the law to the needs of the time. He considered that codification was not so successful in practice as it sounded in theory. It was very difficult, if not impossible, to draft a statute to cover all circumstances and consequently so many alterations were required that the original statute was swamped by amendments. He points out that it is bound to take time before a new law is widely known even to lawyers and that an established law known to everyone is of more use and convenience to society than a new law which has to be newly learned.[16] These sentiments are echoed down the years by English lawyers, and in 1744 William Murray, later Lord Mansfield said, "A statute can seldom take in all cases, therefore, the common law that works itself pure by rules drawn from the fountain of justice is for this reason superior to an Act of Parliament."[17]

Hale had a great distaste for technicalities in matters of procedure. He complains that the length and niceties of pleadings in his day far exceeded those in the time of Henry VI, Edward IV and Henry VII[18] and points out that the only object of pleadings is "to render the fact plain and intelligible and to bring the matter to judgment with a convenient certainty".[19] It had degenerated into an elaborate game and many good causes were lost because of technical faults in the pleadings. He points out that many technical words and expressions which had a meaning and purpose in days gone by were repeated in pleadings when they had ceased to have any meaning or object and comments on the fact that pleadings were drawn by clerks who had a vested interest in their length as they were paid by the folio.[20] He criticizes the judges for a readiness "to give countenance to frivolous exceptions tho' they make nothing to the true merits of the causes"[21] and would have approved of the practice of the judges of today who will accept amendments to the pleadings even at the hearing if the interests of justice require it.

With regard to the form of indictments Hale accepts the general principle that the criminal should have the benefit of the doubt if he can find a technical fault in the indictment. But he thinks that in his day this strictness had gone too far and that "More offenders escape by the over easy ear given to exceptions in indictments, than by their own innocence, and many times gross murders, burglaries, robberies, and other heinous and crying offences escape by those unseemly niceties to the reproach of the law, to the shame of the government and to the encouragement of villainy, and to the dishonour of God."[22] The criticisms are levelled at the administration of justice in his own day but are equally valid at any period of history. To Hale it was just as important that the guilty should be convicted as that the innocent should be cleared and that the law was defective if the guilty were allowed to go free.

He was quick to detect any abuse of the process of the court and had a low opinion of many attornies who brought the law into disrepute by using tricks to delay and pervert justice. He was equally short with members of the bar who sought to hide the truth and thought that the procedure by way of writ of error lent itself to abuse.

Hale had the common lawyer's distrust of written evidence and preferred the English system of oral evidence in open court. In his panegyric on trials by jury in *The History of the Common Law* Chapter VII, he says that when the evidence is given on oath in open court in the presence of the parties, their counsel, judge, jury and bystanders it can speedily be questioned. If a judge is partial this is immediately apparent to the bystanders and if he makes a mistake in the law any party can appeal by way of writ of error. Evidence is given openly in public by word of mouth and subject to cross-examination. A jury is not bound to accept the evidence given in open court and can give their verdict on the evidence of one witness a thing which the civil law will not permit. Hale felt that this method of trial was the best available to find out the facts in a disputed matter, but he was also concerned with judicial standards and there was nothing better for judicial behaviour than a trial in public.

The subject of good faith and keeping one's word frequently occurs in Hale's thinking. In his private affairs he was scrupulous to keep the oath that he made in youth not to take part in toasting. In his treatise on natural law he stresses the sanctity of contract and the necessity for a man to keep his part of any contract into which he voluntarily enters. A judge swears to do justice in accordance with law and it is this binding oath which compels him to give judgment in accordance with the law, however distasteful the consequences may be. This principle is as binding on the king as on his subjects and at his coronation he swears to observe the laws and preserves the liberties of his subjects. It is essential for the king to keep this oath as if he does not do so he destroys the mutual confidence between king and subjects. Without such confidence the people become apprehensive about their property, business confidence is sapped and enterprize is damped down.[23] The principle of good faith is particularly important in business dealings and is one of the basic concepts of the common law which was used to great effect to develop our commercial law in the eighteenth century.

Hale exemplifies all the attributes which the public thinks a good judge should have, except speed. He was learned, experienced and thorough; honest and incorruptible, impartial and objective, patient and courteous to all. He thought time was well spent if the right conclusion was reached. As a judge he concerned himself not only with his judicial duties but also with the other functions of a judge relating to legal education and law reform. He was an expounder of the law to the king and his Ministers, the students, the practitioners and the public. His passion for truth drove him back to the ancient records to find out what they actually said and he refused to rely on copies which were likely to be faulty. His high standards both of behaviour and scholarship were of particular value when it was not uncommon to misread evidence and quote

M

precedents falsely. Holdsworth says: "His character and talents made him easily the greatest English lawyer of his day. His association with the school of historical jurists of whom Selden was the chief, made him with the exception of Francis Bacon the most scientific jurist that England had yet seen. At the same time his active life as a barrister and a judge during the troubled period of the Rebellion and the Commonwealth made him an acute political thinker."[24] He was influenced by the spirit of scientific inquiry which characterized the mental outlook of his age and did not accept the opinion of his contemporaries on public law but formed his own views after studying the historical evidence.

Hale fully understood the complexities of the human situation and the difficulties of arriving at the truth. His own motto, *"Festina Lente"*, shows his attitude to the search for truth and that time was well spent if the true facts were established and the parties were satisfied that justice had been done.

NOTES

1   James R. Cameron, *Frederic William Maitland and the History of English Law*, p. 15.
2   F. W. Maitland, "Why the History of English Law is not Written", *Collected Papers*, vol. I, p. 486.
3   Matthew Hale, *The History of the Common Law*, 3rd ed. 1736, p. 8.
4   F. W. Maitland, "Why the History of English Law is not Written", *Collected Papers*, vol. I, p. 491.
5   Thirwall, vol. I, p. 157.
6   Holdsworth, *A History of English Law*, vol. V, p. 503.
7   ibid., p. 504.
8   *Collectanea Juridica*, p. 267.
9   Hale, *The History of the Common Law*, p. 67.
10 ibid., p. 68.
11 ibid., p. 69.
12 Thirlwall, vol. I, p. 167.
13 Viscount Radcliffe, *Not in Feather Beds*, 1968, p. 271.
14 Hale, *The History of the Common Law*, p. 44.
15 Hargrave, *Tracts*, vol. II, p. 260.
16 *Collectanea Juridica*, p. 267.
17 Omychund *v.* Barker (1744), 1 Atkins Reports, p. 33.
18 Hale, *History of the Common Law*, p. 172.
19 ibid., p. 172.
20 ibid., p. 174.
21 ibid., p. 174.
22 Hale, *The History of the Pleas of the Crown*, 1st ed., vol. II, p. 193.
23 Holdsworth, *A History of English Law*, vol. V, p. 511.
24 Holdsworth, *A History of English Law*, vol. VI, p. 581.

BIBLIOGRAPHY

Aiken, John, *The Lives of John Selden and Archbishop Usher*, Matthews and Leigh, London, 1812.

Anonymous, *A Tryal of Witches at the Assizes held at Bury St. Edmunds taken by a person attending the court*, William Shrewsbury, London, 1682.

Atkyns, Robert, *The Ancient and Present State of Gloucestershire*, 2nd Ed., London, 1712.

Aubrey, John, *Brief Lives*, ed. Andrew Clarke, O.U.P., 1898, vol. I.

Baxter, Richard, *Reliquiae Baxterianae*, ed. Matthew T. Parkhurst and others, London, 1696.

Baxter, Richard, *The Certainty of the Worlds of Spirits*, London, 1691.

Bell, Walter George, *The Great Fire of London in 1666*, John Lane, Bodley Head, London, 1920.

Birch, Thomas, *The Life of Dr John Tillotson*, London, 1753.

Burnet, Gilbert, *Lives of Sir Matthew Hale and John Earl of Rochester*, William Pickering, London, 1829. 1682 ed. Wing B5828 £15(1978 Hannas)

Burnet, Gilbert, *History of His Own Time*, ed. Osmund Airy, vol. I, O.U.P., 1897.

Burton, Thomas, *Diary*, vols. I and III, London, 1828.

Cameron, James R., *Frederic William Maitland and the History of English Law*, Norman University of Oklahoma Press, 1961.

Campbell, John Lord, *The Lives of the Chief Justices of England*, vol. I, John Murray, London, 1858.

Collectanea Juridica, vol. I, E. and R. Brooke, London, 1791 (containing Hale's preface to Rolle's *Abridgment*).

Commons Journal, vol. VII.

Cottrell, Mary, "The Hale Commission of 1652", *English Historical Review*, October 1968, vol. LXXXIII, p. 690.

Davies, R. T., *Four Centuries of Witch Beliefs*, Methuen and Co., London, 1947.

Eden, Sir Frederic Morton, *The State of the Poor*, George Routledge and Son Ltd, 1928.

Ewen, C. L'Estrange, *Witch Hunting and Witch Trials*, Kegan Paul, London, 1929.

Foss, Edward, *The Judges of England*, vol. VII, 1864.

Foster, Joseph, *Alumni Oxoniensis 1500–1714*, vol. II.

Haller, William, *The rise of Puritanism*, Columbia University Press, 1938.

Hargrave, Francis, *A Collection of Tracts Relating to the Law of England*, vol. I, T. W. Wright, London, 1787.

Havinghurst, Alfred F., "The Judiciary in the Reign of Charles II", *Law Quarterly Review*, 1950, vol. 66, p. 62.

Hearsey, John E. N., *London and the Great Fire*, John Murray, London, 1965.

Henderson, P. A. Wright, *The Life and Times of John Wilkins*, William Blackwood and Sons, Edinburgh and London, 1910.

Hill, Christopher, *The Century of Revolution 1603–1714*, Thomas Nelson and Sons Ltd, Edinburgh, 1961.

Hill, Christopher, *Society and Puritanism*, Secker and Warburg, 1964.

Hill, Christopher, *Puritanism and Revolution*, Secker and Warburg, 1958.

Hill, Christopher, *Economic Problems of the Churches from Archbishop Whitgift to the Long Parliament*, O.U.P., 1956.

Hobbes, Thomas, *The Elements of Law National and Politic*, ed. Ferdinand Tonnies, C.U.P., 1928.

Holdsworth, William S., *A History of English Law*, vols. I and VI, Methuen, London, 1924.

Holdsworth, William S., "Sir Matthew Hale", *Law Quarterly Review*, 1923, vol. 39, p. 402.

Howell, T. B., (ed.), *Complete Collection of State Trials*, London, 1812.

Hutchinson, Francis, *An Historical Essay Concerning Witchcraft*, London, 1720.

Jones, Philip E., (ed.), *The Fire Court*, vol. I, William Clowes and Son Ltd, 1966.

Kittredge, G. L., *Witchcraft in Old and New England*, Harvard University Press, 1929.

Laslett, Peter, *The World We Have Lost*, Methuen, London, 1965.

Lindley, E. S., *Wotton under Edge*, Museum Press, 1962.

Leonard, E. M., *The Early History of English Poor Relief*, C.U.P., 1900.

Lloyd, David, *State Worthies*, vol. II, London, 1766.

Lysons, David, *The Environs of London*, vol. II, London, 1795.

Maitland, Frederic William, *Collected Papers*, ed. H. A. L. Fisher, vols. I and II, C.U.P., 1911 "Why the History of English Law is not Written", vol. I, p. 480. "The Materials for English Legal History", vol. II, p. 5.

Markham, Clement R., *A Life of the Great Lord Fairfax*, Macmillan, London, 1870.

Marlowe, John, *The Puritan Tradition in English Life*, The Cresset Press, London, 1956.

Neal, Daniel, *The History of the Puritans*, vol. IV, Brice Edmond, Dublin, 1755.

North, Roger, *The Autobiography of The Hon. Roger North*, London, 1887.

North, Roger, *The Lives of Francis North, Dudley North and John North*, vol. I, George Bell and Sons, London, 1890.

Notestein Wallace, *A History of Witchcraft in England from 1588–1718*, O.U.P., 1911.

Nourse, G. B., "Law Reform under the Commonwealth and Protectorate", *Law Quarterly Review*, Oct. 1959, vol. 75, p. 518.

Oman, Carola, *Elizabeth of Bohemia*, Hodder and Stoughton, London, 1964.

Phillimore, W. P. W., *Gloucestershire Parish Registers*, vol. X, London, 1905.

Phillips, Margaret Mann, *Erasmus on his Times*, C.U.P. Paperback, 1967.

Plucknett, T. F. T., "Maitland's View of Law and History", *Law Quarterly Review*, 1951, vol. LXVII, p. 179.

Pocock, J. G. A., *The Ancient Constitution and the Feudal Law*, C.U.P., 1957.

Pollock, Sir Frederick and Frederic Maitland, *The History of English Law*, 2nd ed., vol. II, C.U.P., 1968.

Powicke, Frederick J., *The Rev. Richard Baxter under the Cross 1662–1691*, Jonathan Cape, London, 1927.

Prall, Stuart E., *The Agitation for Law Reform during the Puritan Revolution 1640–1660*, Martinus Nijhoff, The Hague, 1966.

Purver, Margery, *The Royal Society: Concept and Creation*, Routledge and Kegan Paul, London, 1967.

Radcliffe, Viscount, *Not in Feather Beds*, Hamish Hamilton, 1968.

Rigg, J. M., *Dictionary of National Biography*, vol. VIII, 1908.

Roberts, Clayton, *The Growth of Responsible Government in Stuart England*, C.U.P., 1966.

Rolle, Henry, *Abridgment*, London, 1668.

Roscoe, Henry, *Lives of Eminent British Lawyers*, Longman Green, London, 1830.

Runnington, Charles, *Some account of the life of Sir Matthew Hale being a preface to the 5th Edition of The History of the Common Law by Matthew Hale*, G. C. and J. Robinson, London, 1794.

Smith, Sir Hubert Llewellyn, *The Board of Trade*, G. P. Putnam and Sons Ltd, London, 1928.

Somers, J. S., *Collection of Tracts*, 2nd ed., vols. VI and XI, John Murray, London, 1814.

Stein, Peter, *Regulae Juris From juristic rules to legal maxims*, Edinburgh University Press, 1966.

Thurloe, *State Papers*, vols. IV and V.

Tullock, John, *English Puritanism and its leaders*, William Blackwood and Sons, Edinburgh, 1859.

Turner, Edward Raymond, *The Privy Council of England in the 17th and 18th Centuries 1603–1784*, The John Hopkins Press, vol. II, London, 1928.

Wedgwood, C. V., *Thomas Wentworth First Earl of Stafford*, Jonathan Cape, London, 1961.

Williams, J. B., *Memoirs of the Life, Character and Writing of Sir Matthew Hale*, Jackson and Walford, London, 1835.

Wood, Anthony, *Athenae Oxoniensis*, vol. II, R. Knaplock, D. Midwinter and J. Tomson, London, 1721.

APPENDIX

APPENDIX A

Published Books on Law by Matthew Hale

Preface to Rolle's Abridgment, London, 1668. Also appears in *Collectanea Juridica*, vol. I, no. IX, p. 266–7.

A Short treatise touching Sheriffs' Accompts, London, 1683.

The History of the Pleas of the Crown, 1st ed., ed. Sollom Emlyn, vols. I and II, London, 1736.

The History of the Common Law, 3rd Ed., London, 1739.

The Analysis of the Law, 3rd Ed., London, 1739. (Published with *The History of the Common Law*.)

A Treatise in three parts on Rivers, Ports, and concerning the custom of goods imported and exported. Francis Hargrave's *Tracts*, vol. I, p. 1, London, 1787.

Considerations touching the Amendment or Alteration of laws, Hargrave's *Tracts*, vol. I, p. 249.

Discourse concerning the Courts of King's Bench and Common Pleas, Hargrave's *Tracts*, vol. I, p. 357.

The Jurisdiction of the Lord's House or Parliament considered according to ancient records, ed. Francis Hargrave, London, 1796.

Anthony Fitzherbert's New Natura Brevium with commentary by Sir Matthew Hale, 8th ed., London, 1755.

Sir Edward Coke's First Institute of the Laws of England with commentary by Sir Matthew Hale, ed. Francis Hargrave, 14th ed., London, 1789.

Summary of the Pleas of the Crown, London, 1682.

APPENDIX B

Hale Manuscripts at British Museum

1. Treatise on Maritime Law 1667. Add. MS. 30228. This is the treatise published by Francis Hargrave on rivers, ports and customs. Hargrave's *Tracts* vol. I, p. 1.
2. Two identical manuscripts on the powers of the king entitled:

Extracts from treatise on English Government. Add MS. 14291 f.222.

On the laws of England. Lansdown MS. 632.

3. Two identical manuscripts on the amendment of the law entitled: Treatise on the laws of England. Add. MS. 18234.

On the amendment of English laws. Harl MS. 4990 Art 2.

Published in Hargrave's *Tracts*, vol. I, p. 249.

4. Two identical manuscripts on Hale's reply to Hobbes entitled: Reflections on Hobbe's dialogue "De corpore politico". Add MS. 18235 f.2.

Reflections on Hobbe's dialogue. Harl MS. 4990 Art. 1.

Printed in Holdsworth's *A History of English Law*, vol. V. Appendix III.

5. Two identical manuscripts on natural law entitled: Treatise on the Law of Nature. Add. MS. 18325 f.41.

Tract on Natural Law. Harl MS. 7159 Art. 1.

6. Three lists of MSS. given to Lincoln's Inn.

Index to his MSS. in Lincoln's Inn by J. Hunter, 19th century. Add. MS. 25471.

Catalogue of his MSS. Harl MS. 6030 Art. 6.

Lists of MSS. given to Lincoln's Inn, 1676. Stowe MS. 1056 f.86.

7. Arguments and notes 1669. Add. MSS. 35994 f.61; 36086 f.1.

8. Statement as to the property of W. Platt in the time of Charles I. Add. MS. 38091 f.120.

9. Arguments relating to Court of Marches in Wales 1660. Add. MS. 41661 ff.156–72.

10. Treatise on Sheriffs' Accompts, 17th century. Add. MS. 41661 ff.192b–216. This was published as *A Short Treatise Touching Sheriffs' Accompts*, London, 1683.

11. Argument in Collingwood *v.* Pace 1664. Add. MS. 41661 ff.216–27.

12. Tract on enrolment of deeds 1668. Add. MS. 41661 ff. 216–27.

Published in Somers *Tracts*, vol. IV, p. 81.

13. Two identical copies of History of the Common Law entitled: History of the Common Law. Harl MS. 711 Art. 1 and Harl MS. 7160 Art. 1.

An extract only from the History. Stowe MS. 163 f.146. Third edition published 1739.

14. On the succession. Harl MS. 4666 Art. 1.

15. On the powers of English Kings, 1657. Sloane MS. 1435 ff.107–21b.

16. Concerning the secondary origination of mankind by natural propagation. Add. MS. 9001.

17. Letters to his grandchildren. Harl MS. 4009 Art. 1.

18. Medical case, 1676. Stowe MS. 745 f.117.

19. Two identical manuscripts on the Admiralty jurisdiction. Hargrave MSS. 137 and 93.

20. Minutes of the Hale Commission, 1652. Hardwick Papers B.M. Add. MSS. 35863.

INDEX